WORK TEAMS:
STORIES TO HELP MANAGE THEM

BY FRANK DOERGER

WHITMORE PUBLISHING CO.
PITTSBURGH, PENNSYLVANIA 15222

Whitmore Publishing Co.
701 Smithfield Street
Pittsburgh, PA 15222
Visit our website at *www.whitmorebooks.com*

ISBN: 978-1-4809-0572-6

INTRODUCTION

This collection of anecdotes is designed to remind you of management principles you may forget to practice. The setting for the anecdotes is a breakfast club attended by a group of managers employed by large and small businesses and hospitals. The members share the "minutes" with managers in their organizations.

I hope you find this collection helpful and entertaining.

TABLE OF CONTENTS

CURSE OF KNOWLEDGE

"Get this," announced a member as she joined our meeting. "I mentioned William W. Scherkenbach to my boss, and he hadn't even heard of him!"

The dead silence indicated that none of us were familiar with the name.

"Ah, the curse of knowledge," announced another member. Continued silence and confused looks prompted an explanation.

Our team member reminded us that, once we know something, it's difficult to imagine what it is like to not know it. This "curse of knowledge" is the root of many workplace problems. By assuming others know exactly what we know, we shortcut our verbal and written communication but assume we communicated well. Then, when things don't go right, we become frustrated and may even be tempted to accuse people (especially those in other departments) of being naïve, lazy, or thick headed!

There is no simple solution, especially in an era of job specialization, innumerable acronyms, and life in the information age.

Managers must be aware of "the curse of knowledge" and develop a culture that encourages people to speak up when they don't understand something.

ᔕᙖᔕ

WHO TOOK MY LUNCH?

"Darn it," announced a member as she joined our meeting. "Again, someone stole my lunch out of the department's refrigerator."

There was a suspicious lack of interest or concern from the team members. It was easy to assume those in the meeting had at least once committed such a dastardly act!

In fact, our friends in human resources indicate that stolen lunches and drinks are a common complaint in all industries. Some consultants say such pilfering lowers morale. Some say it may be an indicator of low morale.

A behavioral economist did a study of college dorms with communal refrigerators. He placed six packs of soft drinks in the refrigerators to see how long they would go "unstolen." All were gone within seventy-two hours.

He then tried something similar with money left in the open. It was not taken. He theorized that we find it easy to rationalize taking "things" versus taking money.

⌒≈⌐

As Good As It Gets

"On my way to this meeting," announced a Breakfast Club member as she joined us, "I overheard an associate paraphrase a line from a movie." She teased several of her co-workers with the remark: "Just think, this may be as good as it gets in this department!"

That prompted the Breakfast Club members to discuss team morale. We agreed that it, like most things in life, invariably has its ups and downs. We also agreed it is the manager's role to be aware of the team's mood and respond accordingly. So, when the team is down, absorb that mood but reflect it back to them with words or actions which demonstrate your continued sense of optimism. That informs the team you know how they feel, but it also gives them the little boost they need and probably expect from you.

A prime function of a leader is to keep hope alive.
- John W. Gardner

⌒≈⌐

Aha!

"I had an 'aha' last night at the open house held at my ten-year-old's elementary school," announced a member as he joined our meeting.

"Share your newly found wisdom," responded another member.

"Well, I'm embarrassed to admit our emphasis on diversity has long perplexed me. I guess I didn't really understand what was meant by diversity or what we were expected to do. It hit me when I saw a poster in the school's hall."

He then wrote this on the white board:

D ifferent
I ndividuals
V aluing

E ach other
R egardless of
S kin
I ntellect
T alents or
Y ears

～⌒～

CAN YOU REPEAT THAT?

"Thank goodness for cell phones," announced a member as she joined our meeting.

"My daughter, who lives in Columbus, and I were to meet for lunch at a Bob Evans about midway between Cincinnati and Columbus. I know I was very specific about which Bob Evans. After waiting and worrying for twenty-five minutes, I called her cell phone. She was waiting for me at another Bob Evans!"

All of us had stories of "clear, straightforward communication" that turned out to be anything but.

Since we already are familiar with the message we are sending, it's easy for us to assume it's clear to the listener. But studies show that communications between people who speak the same language are not understood 12.5 percent of the time, and the rate goes up in high-stress situations.

Repeating our message or asking the recipient to state his/her understanding of it may be well worth the effort.

> *If you had listened hard enough, you might have heard what I meant to say.*
>
> - Rod McKuen

～⌒～

CAN YOU SEE ME NOW?

"I walked down the hall with a manager and felt like a character in the novel *Invisible Man*," announced a member as she joined our meeting.

"The Ellison or Wells book?" asked our English Lit major.

"Both," was the reply.

We learned that the manager saw several associates who report to him but totally ignored them as they passed by. No hello, no smile, no eye contact.

"He acted like they were invisible," stated our member.

We agreed that feeling "important" is a basic human need. And managers can help meet that need in a number of ways. It can be as simple as acknowledging them in the hall, regularly chatting with them, learning about their interests, or joining them for lunch.

We also agreed it is not only the polite thing to do, but it improves morale and retention.

⤫

BREAK THE ICE; MAKE A FRIEND

"Those articles about friendliness saved me two dollars," proudly announced a member as she joined our group.

"They were on my mind as I was doing grocery shopping on Saturday morning. I was in the cereal aisle and decided to be friendly. I said to the elderly lady shopping near me, "Gosh, there are so many kinds of cereals it makes it hard to find the one you want.

"She asked me the name of the brand I was looking for. Not only did she show me where it was, she gave me a coupon worth two dollars!"

We agreed that most people want to be friendly, but many of us have a difficult time taking the initiative to "break the ice." But doing so sometimes ends up in friendships, business contacts, coupons, and even marriage.

⤫

BLAME GAME

"I have a story about thoughtless customers," announced a member as she joined our meeting.

"My husband and I went shopping on Saturday morning. Naturally, we roamed about the mall with cups of coffee in hand. My husband mentioned how many empty cups and soda cans were on benches and tucked in corners. In fact, we overheard a security guard complain about it and how inconsiderate he thought shoppers were."

"We quickly discovered why there was so much litter. We couldn't find a trash can for our coffee cups."

The Breakfast Club members agreed that it's easy to criticize customers when they don't behave as we expect or prefer. We also agreed that it behooves us to take a hard look at our processes before we put all the blame on customers.

⤫

Beat the Competition

"Not long ago my father-in-law retired from a thirty-five year career in management consulting," announced a member as he joined our meeting.

"Of course, that means he'll be visiting my wife and me more often and entertaining us with stories about his many consulting projects.

"He's been involved in Zero Base Budgeting, Management by Objective, Six Sigma, Continuous Quality Management, Quality Circles, Feng Shui, Theory X and Y, and others I'm not familiar with."

Our team member went on to say he asked his father-in-law which approach seemed to be the most effective. He responded with this quote:

"Having great leaders is the ultimate competitive advantage."
- Tom Tiller, CEO, Polaris Corporation

◦⌒◦⌒◦

Begins With a "P"

We asked our members for words that began with the letter "P" which are characteristic of a high-performance team. Here is the final list:

Passion (to lead, to get the job done)
Patience (with others, with time it takes to succeed)
Peaceful (untroubled by conflict)
Peak (striving for perfection)
Peculiar (not afraid to be unconventional)
People (the right mix)
Perfection (strive for)
Persistent (don't give up)
Personality (distinguishing characteristics)
Perspire (hard workers)
Persuasive (able to move others)
Pioneers (preparing for others to follow)
Planning (skills)
Playful (fun at work)
Poised (steady under pressure)
Polite (and friendly)
Positive (attitude, feedback, reinforcement)
Practical (disposed to action)
Pragmatic (problem solvers)
Pray (meditate, reflect, think)
Pride (in work and organization)

Priorities (clearly defined)
Proactive (take the initiative)
Processes (effective, efficient)
Product (viable)
Project (management skills)
Punctual (meeting deadline commitments)
Purpose (clearly defined)
Performance (using data to measure it)
Pflexibility (adapt to new or changing requirements)

※

&*%#$@ (BAD LANGUAGE)

"Yesterday my six-year-old picked up a few new, choice words on the school playground," bemoaned a mother as she joined the Breakfast Club meeting.

"Are you sure he didn't learn them by overhearing a business meeting or two?" asked another member, only half kidding.

The conversation quickly turned to workplace profanity. Two of us were surprised to learn that foul language in meetings is not unheard of. Some claim it is even predictable in some settings.

We agreed that, in rare instances of extreme circumstances and emotions, swearing may come naturally and be excused. But we also agreed that habitual offensive language is bad manners, quickly shuts down communication, creates a bad image, and puts stress on relationships. It can also contribute to a hostile work environment that may result in a lawsuit.

He knew the precise psychological moment when to say nothing.
- Oscar Wilde

※

BACK FROM THE FUTURE

"My fifties kitchen is now complete," announced a member as she joined us. "I added a rotary-dial telephone. And I get a kick out of watching guests try it out."

She told us about young people who had never seen one and didn't know how to use it. She also said adults play with it just to reminisce. Interestingly, adults mentioned its therapeutic effect. Many said, "It forces me to slow down."

We agreed that speed dial, cell phones, pagers, PDAs, email, voice mail, and laptops entice us into a frenetic pace. We fall into the trap of believing that hurrying and constantly planning our next move makes us productive.

The team agreed that slowing down, that deliberateness, that attention to now, helps us do everything even better. And it also helps us be aware of the precious present that often goes by unappreciated and unenjoyed.

Rotary phones, anyone?

P.S.: We can actually use our touch-tone phone to our advantage. Each time we use it, we can ask ourselves: "Does it make sense to slow down?"

> *For unless one is able to live fully in the present, the future is a hoax. There is no point whatever in making plans for a future that you will never be able to enjoy. When your plans mature, you will still be living for some other future beyond.*
>
> - Alan Watts

∽⌘∾

ATTITUDE CHECK

The Breakfast Club members recently discussed team morale. One member wondered how it can be measured and how often it should be measured. "When I was in the military," replied another member, "morale was measured every morning without fail." That got everyone's attention. "Right after roll call," he continued, "the First Sergeant bellowed 'Attitude check!' Everyone was required to yell back: 'This Army is allllll right!'"

Unlike military leaders, we can't control responses, but it does make sense to ask every now and then. An informal approach is to simply to ask how things are going and then pay close attention to the answers.

Another approach is to ask all team members to anonymously pencil their own morale score (on a one to ten scale, where five is average) on a piece of paper. A graphical way is to ask members to draw an arrow—up, down, or sideways. Up means increasing; down means decreasing; and sideways means staying about the same. Discuss the results at the next team meeting.

∽⌘∾

ASK THE CUSTOMER

"I'm feelin' good," declared a member as she bounded into the Breakfast Club meeting.

"Share, before you burst," pleaded another member.

"Two days ago, a work team was trying to decide between two straight-forward options I'll call 'A' and 'B.' The decision would directly impact about twenty internal customers. Everyone, me included, was almost positive option A would be preferred by the customers. However, I suggested we ask them. To everyone's surprise—and to my delight— nineteen out of twenty wanted option B."

The Breakfast Club members agreed that, whenever feasible, the customer should be consulted before a decision is made.

P.S.: Santa Claus has used the "ask the customer" approach for centuries.

⌘

ALL TOGETHER NOW

"My neighbor is on a month-long vacation, which is causing me to gain weight," remarked one of our members.

"Please explain the cause and effect," demanded our taciturn member.

"We exercise together, and without her encouragement, I'm working out less and less."

Her comment reminded a member of this story: In the early 1900s, barges were used to transport goods in China. Each barge was pulled by six men, and they were rewarded handsomely if the goods arrived on time. Each man realized that, as long as the other five pulled steadily, it didn't matter if he took it easy since the team would succeed anyway. So why pull hard? Each man also realized that, if the others did not pull steadily, his strong efforts would not be enough to succeed. So why pull hard?

The six men agreed on a solution. They hired a seventh man whose job it was to whip the shirkers!

It is all too easy to become complacent. That's why encouragement is common in school and sports. We questioned how common it is at work. We agreed one of a manager's responsibilities is to be a good listener and to encourage his or her team and fellow managers.

> *Flatter me, and I may not believe you. Criticize me, and I may not like you. Ignore me, and I may not forgive you. Encourage me, and I will not forget you.*
>
> - William Arthur Ward

⌘

CUSTOMER FOCUSED

"Now this is an example of customer-focused, detailed thinking," announced a Breakfast Club member as he burst into the meeting room. "Look at this copy of *The Old Farmer's Almanac*," he continued as he passed around a few copies.

"Note that a hole is drilled completely through the upper left corner—a clear statement that these magazine folks really understood their original customers."

All he got was perplexed looks.

Do you know why the magazine comes with a hole in it?

P.S.: *The Old Farmer's Almanac* is North America's oldest continuously published periodical. It was started in 1792 with: "Our main endeavor is to be useful, but with a pleasant degree of humour." It comes out every year in September.

❧

AN IDEAL ASSOCIATE

The Breakfast Club members recently discussed the characteristics of the ideal associate—manager and non-manager. We challenged ourselves to come up with the one, single characteristic most valued by employers.

The consensus: always doing what most needs to be done without waiting to be asked. And, since bosses can't be everywhere, bringing to the boss's attention what needs to be done.

❧

AN IDEAL BOSS

"I just read another interesting article about Baptist Hospital in Pensacola, Florida," announced a member as she joined our meeting.

"In every new hire orientation, they ask their new associates: 'What makes a great leader?' They track the responses and share them with managers to help them understand what new associates are looking for in their leaders."

"And survey says?" quipped another member.

Here are the most common responses over an eighteen month period:

Honest
Fair
Good Communicator
Respectful

Consistent
Approachable
Visionary
Flexible
Integrity
Professional
Reward and Recognize
Team Leader/Player
Empathetic
Sense of Humor
Listener
Trustworthy
Understanding

Were you surprised by any that made the list?

❦

APPRECIATION

"Thank goodness for the iPod," announced a member as she joined our meeting.

"Details, please," demanded our taciturn member.

"Friday I returned from visiting my parents. I was on a three-hour flight and two businessmen occupied the seats directly behind me. I couldn't help but overhear their every word."

One of them volunteered for a non-profit organization and had just finished a major project for them. He was proud of the results but in his words, "Not even a thank you note."

The conversation then switched to their employers. They began trading horror stories about impersonal bosses and employers.

"At that point I was getting depressed," continued our team member, "and I hooked up my iPod and drowned them out."

Another member quickly shared a factoid with us. According to the U.S. Department of Labor, the number-one reason people leave their jobs is because...

The answer is later in this book.

❦

First Job

"I spent a lot of the holiday weekend laughing," announced a member as she joined our meeting. She continued, "My son and his two friends, who have been in their first real jobs for just a few months, entertained us with stories about annoying co-workers. The stories, dramatics included, were funny and pathetic at the same time."

She went on to say the young men mentioned annoying habits like incessant whistling, stealing food from the communal refrigerator, finger drumming, taking things without asking, droning on about their love life, listening to the radio and singing aloud to every song, disturbing others by talking too loud, running a business from the office, constant backbiting, signing email with quotes that "push" their religion, goldbricking, not making more coffee when they take the last cup, and many, many more.

The team agreed that each of us would do a little soul searching to see if perhaps we had an annoying habit or two. Others decided to ask their colleagues to alert them if they were consistently doing annoying things.

✂⊱⊰✂

Repeat Customers

"Listen to this customer satisfaction approach," announced a member as she joined our meeting. "My nephew recently joined the management team of a large hotel in New York City. Guests have many hotels to choose from, so repeat business hinges on the quality of the guest's last stay."

She went on to say her nephew educated her on three levels of customer satisfaction. They are:

1. Must Have
2. More is Better
3. Delighters

The Must Haves are the things customers take for granted. They notice their absence more than their presence. If any of the Must Haves is missing the customer is annoyed. In the hotel business, a clean room is a Must Have.

The More is Better category has more flexibility. If the customer's need is poorly met, satisfaction decreases. But satisfaction goes up the better the need is met. In the hotel business, threadbare or fluffy towels are examples.

The Delighters are good surprises. Chocolate mints neatly placed on the pillow or a free newspaper may be examples in the hotel business.

Of course, customers have changing needs and wants. A Delighter on one visit could easily become a Must Have on the next visit.

⌒⦿⌒

ARE YOU LISTENING – REALLY?

Recently the Breakfast Club members were discussing some pet peeves about some of their past managers. We came up with these top five that are really irritating:

Interrupting while the associate is talking: This one seems pretty obvious, but it's easy, given the hectic pace most managers must follow, to jump in when you *think* you know what your staff member is going to say next.

Not making eye contact: If you're not focusing through eye contact, there's a good chance you're not engaged mentally, either. Even if you *are* listening, associates perceive that you're not. But remember, there can be too much of a good thing. You'll appear to be "staring them down" if you hold eye contact too long.

Forgetting to give feedback: When managers don't take the time to give feedback—except when things go wrong—it's difficult for associates to gauge how they're doing.

Ignoring associates while answering the phone: If a staff member is in the office for a meeting and the phone rings, *let voice mail pick it up.* If you answer in the middle of your staff member's comments, it sends the message that whoever's on the phone is more important.

Reading when associate is talking: Short staffing and time constraints are probably forcing you to "multi-task" to get your work done. Resist the impulse to do this while an associate is speaking to you. It's easy to miss certain points of the conversation if you're reading mail and other papers while an associate is explaining something.

⌒⦿⌒

ANSWER THIS

"Darn college kids," announced a member as she joined our group. "They take a week to answer my emails. But, when they want something, they send a dunning email three hours after their request."

"I'm sorry to say, but it sounds like some of our colleagues," added another member.

After the venting ended, we discussed email and voice mail and our organizations' values. We agreed ignoring email and voice mail that requires a response violates them.

However, we couldn't decide on how soon one is expected to respond to email and voice mail.

～∾

CHAIN OF COMMAND

You've probably noticed that the chain of command in most organizations looks something like this:

```
∧ ∧ ∧ ∧ ∧ ∧ ∧ ∧ ∧ ∧ ∧

| | | | | | | | | | | |
| | | | | | | | | | | |
| | | | | | | | | | | |
| | | | | | | | | | | |
```

You've probably also noticed that work gets done like this:

```
∧ ∧ ∧ ∧ ∧ ∧ ∧ ∧ ∧ ∧ ∧

| | | | | | | | | | | |
->->->->->->->->->->->
| | | | | | | | | | | |
| | | | | | | | | | | |
->->->->->->->->->->->
| | | | | | | | | | | |
```

Masao Nemota, managing director of Toyota, told his leaders: "One of the most important functions of a division manager is to improve coordination between his own division and other divisions."

We think it is a big part of every manager's job to connect the vertical lines in the organizational chart.

Masao Nemota closed his pearl of wisdom with: "If you cannot handle this task, please go to work for an American company." Ouch!

～∾

CHANGING AGAIN

"My son, who graduated from college last June, has been in his first real job for just five months. He enjoys his work and has a great relationship with his boss," reported a Breakfast Club member.

"He just learned his boss is being transferred to Japan and a new boss will take over in three weeks. My son is disappointed and also very apprehensive about the change."

We agreed it's natural to be apprehensive, and we came up with these suggestions to help the young man with the transition:

- recognize all management styles are somewhat different
- different does not mean good or bad
- working for people with different styles is a growth experience
- change is not so much a part of business but more so business itself
- learn to "manage up"

⌘

CHECK BEFORE IMPROVING

Several of the Breakfast Club members were riding in a car behind a Metro bus last week. One member suddenly announced, "I'm glad to see the bus manufacturer designed that bus with slowpokes in mind."

Our quizzical looks prompted this explanation: "Early in my working career," she continued, "I took the Metro to work. More mornings than I care to admit, I'd turn the corner and approach my stop just in time to see a bus pulling away. I'd panic and wonder if it was my bus or another that just left. Now, as you can see, they put the bus number on the back of the bus as well as the front."

We agreed all products and services should be designed with ideas from those who actually use them. We also agreed that departments in large organizations such as ours should talk to internal customers before changing procedures that impact them, even indirectly. Sometimes just "improving" a form can cause confusion and unexpected results throughout the organization.

So, how do we identify internal customers? A quick rule of thumb: the next person or department in the process. It's usually a good idea to check with customers several levels deep in the process.

A smart aleck in our group asked: "Is it true the number on the back of the bus is different than the one on the front?"

⌘

CHESS ANYONE?

One of our Breakfast Club members is quite a chess player. He often compares playing chess to being a manager and believes it can take years to feel comfortable at either one.

Beginning chess players often go to great lengths to avoid having any piece taken. By concentrating on saving each piece, they end up losing the game. Experienced players are willing to give up individual pieces as part of an overall strategy that brings victory.

Managers must look at the big picture as well. Perfecting each individual part of a process may not produce the best overall results. In Continuous Quality Improvement parlance, some parts may need to be sub-optimized. For instance, the best customer service reps may be those who actually service fewer customers than average. Their unhurried pace and friendly attitude could increase repeat business or smooth customers' ruffled feathers. Asking them to spend less time on each call could be false economy.

> *"What we need to do is learn to work in the system, by which I mean that everybody, every team, every platform, every division, every component is there not for individual competitive profit or recognition, but for contribution to the system as a whole on a win-win basis."*
>
> - W. Edwards Deming

WHO IS THAT?

A Breakfast Club member shared this story about relationships. She has forgotten where she read this:

A nursing school student attended a class in which the professor gave a pop quiz. She breezed through the questions until she got to the last one. "What is the first name of the woman who cleans the school?"

She immediately thought it was some kind of joke. She had seen the cleaning woman numerous times, but how could she be expected to know her name?

She left the last question blank. As she handed her test to the professor she asked if the last question would count toward her grade.

"Absolutely," the professor said and announced to everyone, "in your careers you will meet many people. All are significant. They deserve your attention, even if all you do is smile or chitchat every now and then."

⌒⌒⌒

COACH

Imagine this: You go to work for one of those new high-flying dot com businesses. It's one with a unique approach to employee retention. During your third week on the job, all new employees are taken by limo to a large football stadium. On the fifty-yard line is a brand new, red Jaguar convertible. An employee is blindfolded and escorted to the thirty-yard line. She is spun around six times and given three small beanbags.

You're told new employees win the car by hitting it with one of the three beanbags. The contestant throws the first beanbag, and her supervisor tells her to make a half turn to the left. She throws the second beanbag and her boss says it landed ten feet short of the car. She hits the car on the third throw and everyone cheers.

You're next. You throw the first beanbag and wait for some guidance from your boss. But you're told he was just called away to an important meeting. You're on your own! It's all over after your next two throws and, needless to say, you don't win the car.

Obviously, good coaching improves performance. On-the-job coaching and sports coaching have a lot in common. Both are:

- done often
- clearly communicated
- open, honest, and accurate
- about specific behavior that can be changed
- encouraging, but refer to productive and unproductive behavior
- non-judgmental

Just like you, your associates are eager to receive good coaching. That's one of the many reasons organizations require a performance review after an associate has been with them for ninety days. Of course, coaching is expected much more frequently.

Not all of us are great coaches like John Wooden, but we can learn from them and from one another. For instance, you may want to periodically ask your associates:

- What do you like best about your job?
- What do you feel most comfortable doing?
- What do you like least about your job?
- What do you feel least comfortable doing?

- How can I help you succeed?

In turn, you may want to bring up specific things you'd like to see them:

- start doing
- continue doing
- stop doing

The idea is to use a structured, yet informal, and comfortable approach to help associates improve.

⌒⌒

COMMITMENT

Do you feel lucky when you have associates who are dedicated to the success of the department? But what makes associates dedicated?

One consulting firm's research found that associates' attitudes and opinions about five key factors determine their level of commitment to an employer. Employees who are loyal to, and likely to remain with, an employer score high in:

Fit and belonging:
- Associates like and get along with one another.
- They feel their interests coincide with the organization's.

Status and identity:
- Associates feel they are part of a special organization.

Trust and reciprocity:
- They feel the organization and its managers can be counted on to do what is good, right, and fair.

Economic interdependence:
- Associates feel they are receiving competitive pay and benefits.

Emotional reward:
- They are satisfied with their jobs, career and development opportunities, and the quality of their work life.

Surprised?

⌒⌒

LET'S COMPLAIN

The Breakfast Club held a meeting on Monday at 8:00 a.m. The early arrivers entertained one another with stories about the crazy way commuters drive. We heard about those who drive too slow, those who drive too fast, those who repeatedly change lanes, those who never change lanes, those who go through yellow lights, and those who don't. "Sounds like we're all complaining about one another," chided one of the participants.

"A bit like what goes on every day at all large organizations," wryly remarked another.

Those comments prompted a lively discussion. It resulted in the Breakfast Club research team being asked to find out why "corporate complaining" is apparently so common.

They gave their report at 3:00 p.m. yesterday. It consisted simply of these words found in the book *The Human Equation, Building Profits by Putting People First* by Jeffrey Pfeffer (Boston: Harvard Business School Press, 1998):

"One of the most widely documented effects in social psychology is the preference of most people to see themselves in a self-enhancing fashion. As a consequence, they regard themselves as more intelligent, skilled, ethical, honest, persistent, original, friendly, reliable, attractive, and fair-minded than their peers or the average person. On the job, approximately ninety percent of managers and workers rate their performance as superior to their peers."

Imagine...there's a good chance those we complain about are complaining about us!

When you catch yourself being judgmental about those within your organization, try this: remind yourself they are also working hard and, like you, probably doing their darndest to get the job done. It just may improve your outlook and your relationships.

❧

CONE OF SILENCE

"Cone of Silence," announced a member as he joined the Breakfast Club meeting.

"I've been a manager for over fifteen years, and I recently learned anew what it is like to be a front-line worker. My daughter is engaged to be married, and my wife has assigned me a few tasks related to the big event."

He then launched into stories, rich with hyperbole and humor, about his tasks.

He claimed to have endured with last-minute changes; lack of tools to do the job; micro-management; unrealistic deadlines; lack of appreciation; nitpicking; a hostile work environment; two bosses (wife and daughter).

After the laughter died down, we agreed that managers should mentally walk in their associates' shoes now and then and remember what it was like before they became a manager.

P.S.: For our younger readers The Cone of Silence is one of many recurring jokes from Get Smart. This 1960s TV comedy series is about an inept spy. Wikipedia has a great description.

⚭

CONVERTING DATA

Prior to the start of last week's Breakfast Club meeting, two members discussed baseball. They disagreed on who were this season's best hitters. A third member naïvely asked if it wasn't simply a matter of batting averages.

The debaters proceeded to educate us on the complexities of baseball statistics. They informed us it is much more than a matter of simple numbers. Additional factors to consider include the size of the home field, whether the home field has natural grass or artificial turf, the person's position in the lineup, injuries, whether or not the home field is "hitter friendly," the quality of opposing pitchers, and the quality of the hitting coaches.

So it is with business statistics. Managers must look for the underlying causes and nuances in the data. As usual, talking to the people closest to the action, the forward observers, is the best way to convert data into information.

It is also a good way to avoid the managerial equivalent of "the man who drowned crossing a stream with an average depth of six inches."

⚭

COPYCAT

"Last night my husband gave me yet another lecture on the history of England's royalty," announced a member as she joined our group.

"Give us the background," blurted another member.

"My husband's new job requires him to regularly travel to London. He uses travel time to read about England. Of course, he's eager to share with me everything he's learned. I must admit I am not as smitten as he is, but one thing he said did intrigue me. Someone asked Queen Elizabeth II how she learned to be queen. She replied, "I learned the way a monkey learns: by watching its parents.""

That prompted a stimulating conversation about a department's culture. We agreed new hires don't read mission statements or codes of proper behavior to find out how to act. They look around and do as others do.

We agreed that one of a manager's primary duties is to set the example that will produce an effective, dedicated, supportive, and friendly team.

> *Grass roots leaders know they must first change their own attitudes and behaviors before expecting their crew to change.*
> - Captain D. Michael Abrashoff

❧

COVER UP

During a Breakfast Club meeting, a member mentioned an article that appeared in the February 2005 issue of *Inc.* magazine.

A public relations manager mailed a set of three golf club covers to numerous clients. It didn't occur to him that some recipients might not know what they were; some didn't. He received notes thanking him for the wine warmers, slippers, and even mittens. (None of the Breakfast Club team members had ever heard of slippers or mittens coming in threes.)

We agreed the moral is especially relevant to the health care industry. Health care can easily be intimidating and confusing, especially to those visiting a hospital for the first time. It is easy for those who work in hospitals to assume everything they do is obvious, even intuitive, to everyone.

❧

CRITICISM

The Breakfast Club members recently discussed criticism in the workplace. We quickly ended up in these camps:

- almost any criticism aimed at improving performance is acceptable
- only constructive criticism is appropriate
- criticism should be avoided at all cost

We challenged the member who espoused absolutely no criticism. Here is her logic:

- criticism is judgmental by nature and weakens relationships
- the criticizer's "facts" may be wrong

- it's often painful to those who are criticized
- it easily causes defensiveness and resentment
- criticism focuses on problems, not solutions
- it can arouse emotions that make it easy for either participant to say the wrong thing

Her recommendation? Privately broach the subject with words like "I'd like us to take a look at how the reports are being prepared and see what's working and not working for both of us." Or, "The data seems to indicate some associates' error rates are way above average. Let's take a look at it and see what we can find out." Or, "I and others have noticed most of your team members are at their work station more regularly than you. How do you see the situation?"

Her tack is the classical win-win approach. The Breakfast Club is going to give it a try.

Honest criticism is hard to take, particularly from a relative, a friend, an acquaintance, or a stranger.
                                                    - Franklin P. Jones

ɷ

Customers are People

"I'm upset with my auto repair shop, can someone recommend a good one?" announced a member as she joined our last meeting.

"Give us the story," replied another member.

"I think they do a good job repairing my car, but I feel like the cashier gives me a cold shoulder and the 'bum's rush' every time I deal with him."

After a few "war stories" about customer service, we assigned our intern to do a little research on customer satisfaction. Her findings:

According to John McKean, a researcher and the author of *Customers are People: The Human Touch*, seventy percent of what determines which company a customer will deal with is based on how humanely they are treated. "What people remember about any interaction is how human or dehumanized they were treated. Were they acknowledged and respected? These things determine if they can trust the company."

He also notes if customers are treated well they will continue to do business with the company, even if that company made a mistake or repeated mistakes.

Interesting stuff. We wondered if the same holds true for the relationship between managers and staff.

DELEGATION

The Breakfast Club recently discussed the art of delegation. We agreed it's easy to entirely avoid delegation with the rationalization "Delegation takes too much time. And delegated work often doesn't get done on time, or if it does, it gets done poorly, and I have to redo it myself." On the other hand, a manager who doesn't master delegation probably ends up spending long, hectic, stressful days at the office. And her staff misses out on the opportunity to learn and grow.

In their book *To Do…Doing…Done!* G. Lynee Snead and Joyce Wycoff suggest that these three ingredients are necessary for effective delegation:

Authority. The person doing the task must have the authority to accomplish it, especially if the task requires additional resources, reprioritization of time, and so on.

Responsibility. Responsibility for the end result is shared by both parties.

Commitment. The person who accepts the task commits to achieving the end result in the agreed-upon time frame.

Sounds like delegation (other than the "dump and run" kind) is really a win-win agreement between boss and helper. And, as with any agreement, detailed up-front discussion is time well spent.

❀

DETAILS, DETAILS, DETAILS

The Breakfast Club discussed how to best prevent things from going wrong. We spent fifteen minutes entertaining one another with Murphy's Law kinds of stories. You know the kind—the fence that's painted a week before it's removed; the stationery that has the corporate logo printed upside down; the company picnic without paper plates.

Those on the outside of the fiasco are quick to ask, "Duh, why didn't they think of that?"

We think Alfred North Whitehead had it right when he said, "We think in generalities, we live in detail." Chances are we usually don't spend quite enough time in the planning stage. Brainstorming in a way that causes details to surface at the beginning of a project can often save many hours and dollars later on.

So, in planning for this year's Breakfast Club picnic, we're going to ask ourselves not only "What needs to be done?" but also "What can go wrong?"

DigiLearning

"I love e-books," announced our techie member as she joined our meeting. She opened her book reader and read this section from Peter F. Drucker's book *The Effective Executive*:

> *"All military services have long ago learned that the officer who has given an order goes out and sees for himself whether it has been carried out. At the least he sends one of his own aides—he never relies on what he is told by the subordinate to whom the order was given. Not that he distrusts the subordinate; he has learned from experience to distrust communications. This is the reason why a battalion commander is expected to go out and taste the food served to his men. He could, of course, read the menus and order this or that item to be brought in to him. But no; he is expected to go into the mess hall and take his sample of the food from the same kettle that serves the enlisted men."*

We agreed it is interesting technology and an interesting managerial concept.

✂✂✂

Why Me?

"Take my husband—please!" announced a Breakfast Club member with a wry smile.

"Give us the story," replied another member as he grinned and raised his eyebrows in anticipation.

"Well, my dear husband retired two months ago. Keep in mind he has never shown any interest in cooking. When I got home last night he proudly announced that he had rearranged the pantry and kitchen cabinets for me! I used to easily find things—no longer."

"Sounds like he needs to attend a class on Continuous Quality Improvement," volunteered a member. "He'll learn that everyone participating in a process, especially the customer, must be involved in redesigning it."

"We better sign him up before he starts on your clothes closet," laughed another member.

P.S.: For our younger readers, "Take my husband—please" is a take-off on Henny Youngman's line "Take my wife—please." Youngman, "King of the One-Liners," was known for his simple rapid-fire jokes, sometimes telling over fifty jokes in an eight minute routine. "Take my wife—please," became so popular it is included in Bartlett's *Familiar Quotations*.

∽◇◇∾

PROFILE OF A DREAM TEAM

- Works toward a common goal
- Develops its members' skills
- Efficiently uses its time and talents
- Embraces the diversity of its members
- Is committed to continuous improvement
- Builds morale internally
- Performs effectively and produces results
- Accepts praise and criticism
- Cooperates rather than competes
- Maintains a positive attitude toward everyone's ideas
- Stays on task
- Uses resources wisely
- Communicates openly
- Teaches and learns from one another
- Resolves conflicts effectively
- Welcomes challenges
- Shares pride in its accomplishments
- Celebrates successes

∽◇◇∾

EDDIE?

"My twelve-year-old son invited his new friend to join us for dinner last night. I can't remember the last time I felt so uncomfortable," announced a member as she joined our meeting.

"We're all ears," responded another member.

"The young man focused the conversation on me with numerous ingratiating questions. He reminded me of Eddie Haskell.

"The kicker went something like this:

"'What's your job at the hospital Mrs. R?'

"'That sounds like a very, very important position.'

"'How do you spend your day?'

"'Gee, the job and the things you spend your time on don't seem to match!'"

We agreed it's easy to get so tangled up in day-to-day details that we lose sight of our real mission. We also agreed it might help if we periodically ask ourselves "What is my job? How am I spending my time?"

P.S.: For our younger readers, Eddie Haskell was an obnoxious teenager on the very popular "Leave It to Beaver" television show that aired from 1957 to 1963. His two trademarks were acting overly polite to adults and goading classmates into trouble that he seemed always to escape.

⌒⌒⌒

Face to Face

A member asked us to write about how the information and communications revolution is affecting our roles as managers. Some members of the Breakfast Club wondered how we ever managed to get along without personal computers, the Internet, Intranet, voice mail, e-mail, pagers, laptops, and smart phones. We asked ourselves if these tools have actually improved communication in organizations. The answer was a definite "yes" and "no."

They have certainly made sending and receiving data, memos, meeting minutes, and newsletters extremely quick and easy. But electronic communication has a significant disadvantage when it comes to more personal matters. It doesn't convey posture, gestures, facial expressions, or voice inflection. And experts tell us that such body language accounts for a large part of communication.

It's very tempting to use e-mail to try to resolve misunderstandings, differences, or conflicts. But in our attempt to avoid an unpleasant or awkward encounter, we often do more harm than good. E-mail can't provide the "real time" give and take that helps us reach a mutual understanding. Nor can it convey a sincere look, a nodding head, or an unexpected smile. And emoticons like :) or ☹ are feeble substitutes. In addition, it doesn't help if the recipient suspects others received a blind copy of the writer's side of the story.

We think old-fashioned person-to-person talking ("face time?") is still the best way to handle some situations.

⌒⌒⌒

Reminders

"Hey, I had the opportunity to talk to Captain Mike Abrashoff," announced a member as she joined our meeting.

"You remember him. He wrote *It's Your Ship: Management Techniques from the Best Damn Ship in the Navy,*" she continued.

"He was the keynote speaker at a national conference I attended, and I chatted with him after his speech. In passing, he mentioned that while he commanded his ship he carried in his wallet a short list of reminders to help him in his everyday leadership duties."

We agreed it is all too easy to let urgent duties come before the really important ones, and a short list of reminders can help us stay on track.

Some of us find it helpful to regularly ask ourselves if we reflect these characteristics:

- Honest
- Fair
- A Good Communicator
- Respectful
- Consistent
- Approachable
- Visionary
- Flexible
- Integrity
- Professional
- Reward and Recognize
- Team Leader/Player
- Empathetic
- Sense of Humor
- Listener
- Trustworthy
- Understanding

∽✑✑∽

FEEDBACK FOR IMPROVEMENT

"I think I'm just about over the 'constructive criticism' I received in my recent performance evaluation," announced a member as he joined our meeting.

"Sounds like someone is suffering from a case of psychosclerosis," blurted another member.

We learned that Ashley Montague coined the word and defined it as the hardening of the attitude which causes a person to cease dreaming, seeing, thinking, and leading.

We agreed any criticism, even well-deserved constructive criticism, is hard to swallow. But we also agreed "feedback for improvement" (we dislike the word criticism) from the right people served the right way helps us focus our attention on what we need to do to be more effective and successful.

> *It is a curious fact that of all the illusions that beset mankind none is quite so curious as that tendency to suppose that we are mentally and morally superior to those who differ from us in opinion.*
>
> - Elbert Hubbard

FEEDBACK

The Breakfast Club members recently discussed feedback. We agreed it is one of a manager's most effective ways to improve individual and group performance. We also agreed it is one of the most underutilized tools.

We're sure that doesn't surprise anyone. After all, who enjoys hearing about their shortcomings? And how many managers look forward to pointing them out to subordinates?

We dislike giving and getting feedback because it's easily interpreted as criticism. And not many relationships can endure criticism.

In his book *Control Theory*, William Glasser, M.D., recommended that discussions aimed at improving performance start something like this: "I want to take a look at what we are both doing in this situation to see where it is working and where it isn't." He suggests talking it through until you agree on something each of you could do to improve matters. The approach makes sense to us because it is nonjudgmental, uses conversational give and take, and results in an action plan.

Of course, positive feedback is important too. It is especially helpful in preventing gains from being lost to old habits. A good rule of thumb is to make sure that positive feedback exceeds negative feedback by four to one. A simple "This is working better for me—thanks for your efforts" from manager or subordinate solidifies the improvement.

Charles Schwab put it this way: "I have yet to find the man, however exalted his station, who did not do better work and put forth greater effort under spirit of approval, than under the spirit of criticism."

FINDING OUR VALUES

A few meetings ago our resident gadfly blurted out, "How come corporations and organizations have this sudden interest in values?"

Of course, we did what any self-respecting team does. We assigned our resident the task of doing the research and presenting the findings at our next meeting. (No sense giving the whippersnapper too much time.) Not only that, we asked that the report be no more than four paragraphs long.

The report consisted of these quotes:

> *The reason leaders must mediate values is that corporations have reached such levels of complexity that "giving orders" rarely works anymore. What increasingly happens is that leaders "manage culture" by fine-tuning values and dilemmas, and then that culture runs the organization. The leader defines excellence and develops an appropriate culture, and then the culture does the excelling.*
>
> - Fons Trompenaars and Charles Hampden-Turner

> *Set your expectations high; find men and women whose integrity and values you respect; get their agreement on a course of action; and give them your ultimate trust.*
>
> - John Fellows Akers

~~~

FISH STORY

"Fish story," announced a member as he joined our meeting.

"On Saturday I spent most of the day fishing with my eighty–year-old father-in-law. Of course, he did the talking, and I was glad to do the listening.

"He spoke a great deal about his long working career. He had stories about great employers, interesting projects, fun co-workers, and giant advances in business practices. I was beginning to feel envious because he was so upbeat. I asked him if he was ever frustrated at work.

"His reply, 'Every day, son, every day.'"

The Breakfast Club members agreed that although work is one of life's potentially most rewarding experiences, along with it comes frustration. It seems organizations are either moving too slow or too fast for us; managers give either too much or too little feedback; co-workers are either too friendly or not friendly enough; business is either too good or not good enough; and on and on.

Most of today's jobs require greater frustration tolerance, personal discipline, organization, management, and interpersonal skills than were required two decades and more ago.

- James P. Comer

∽∾∽

Fix It Before It's Too Late

"My husband and I plan to move to a smaller house, so we're busy landscaping and painting and fixing up our current house," remarked a member as she joined our meeting.

She continued, "We feel like we're doing things we should have done a long time ago. The new owner, not us, will benefit from our recent flurry of improvements."

We agreed it is a common approach to moving. We also agreed it is a good idea to review our work environment through the eyes of a hypothetical "new owner." Then make the improvements that benefit us now.

∽∾∽

Flow

Theory Y managers believe work can be generally rewarding. Some on the Breakfast Club members went so far as to say it has the potential to be one of life's most consistently rewarding experiences. That started a vigorous conversation. It resulted in the Breakfast Club research team being asked to look into the topic and prepare a report.

They used the books of Mihaly Csikszentmihalyi as their primary source. He did extensive research on what he called "flow." You've probably experienced flow. It's when we're in harmony with the world and ourselves. We lose track of time so that hours slip by as if they were minutes. Athletes, artists, and musicians use words such as ecstasy, rapture, and "in the zone" to describe it. It's when "what we feel, what we wish, and what we think" are in harmony. Flow is clearly one of life's most enjoyable experiences.

Dr. Csikszentmihalyi, affectionately referred to as "The Flow Man" by the Breakfast Club members, used an ingenious approach to measure flow. He devised a "happiness scale" of one to seven. One is unhappy and seven is very happy. He gave volunteers a logbook and a pager. The pager went off at random intervals and when it did, volunteers recorded their happiness number and what they were doing at the time.

With apologies to "The Flow Man," we'll try to summarize his research into a few sentences. He looked at all the data and divided activities into three categories: productive activities (like working or studying); maintenance activities (like housework, eating, driving); and leisure activities (like watching TV, reading, playing sports, resting).

He looked at the activities volunteers were engaged in when they reported being in flow. He then determined what those activities had in common.

Briefly, flow seems to occur most often when we are fully engaged in achieving a clear, short-term goal that is neither too easy nor too hard. Too easy and we become bored. Too hard and we become frustrated. There's more to it of course, but generally speaking, sports, hobbies, and — here's the kicker — WORK, offer the most opportunities for flow.

༺༻

FOCUS

The Breakfast Club took a stab at defining the single most important characteristic of associates. We challenged our intern to uncover a quotation related to managers. She presented us with this one from an article in the *Harvard Business Review* by Heike Bruch and Sumantra Ghoshal:

> *"Managers are not paid to make the inevitable happen. In most organizations, the ordinary routines of business chug along without much managerial oversight. The job of managers, therefore, is to make the business do more than chug - to move it forward in innovative, surprising ways."*

They went on to say they've concluded, based on their research, that managers who take effective action rely on a combination of two traits: focus and energy.

༺༻

NAIL

A Breakfast Club member recently sighed "For want of a nail..." Our young intern was perplexed and asked what she meant.

Our member gave her famous "everything is part of a process" lesson. We'll sum it up this way: organizations consist of innumerable, interrelated processes, and many problems are self-inflicted because we change a process without fully understanding how other processes will be affected. (In medical terminology, the side effects.)

For example, changing paper suppliers to save a few cents per hundred sheets could cause an increase in printer jams. In our business, speeding up the patient registration process by asking fewer questions could decrease the amount we are paid for our services.

It is surprisingly easy to "improve" a process and accidentally cause cost increases in other parts of the organization. It is also surprisingly difficult to see the cause and effect. After all, few processes are completely understood by any one person.

Systems theorist Russell L. Ackoff suggests: "To manage a system effectively, you might focus on the interactions of the parts rather than their behavior taken separately."

P.S.: Here's the entire nursery rhyme:
> For want of a nail, the shoe was lost;
> For want of a shoe, the horse was lost;
> For want of a horse, the rider was lost;
> For want of a rider, the battle was lost;
> For want of a battle, the kingdom was lost;
> And all from the want of a horseshoe nail.

∽✦∽

FORCE FIELD ANALYSIS

Two members of the Breakfast Club enjoy quizzing one another on the meanings of acronyms. One mentions the acronym (like SMSA; DRG; PPS; and SNAFU) and the other gives the definition. FFA was brought up during a discussion of process improvement techniques. "Force Field Analysis" was the quick response.

The many blank stares prompted this primer: workplace situations are the way they are for very fundamental reasons called driving and restraining forces. In the case of patient satisfaction scores on a unit, driving forces (forces exerting upward pressure on the scores) may include caring staff. Restraining forces (forces exerting downward pressure on the scores) may include excessive noise. Of course, there are numerous driving and restraining forces and all of them fluctuate in intensity.

So, here's one approach to improving customer satisfaction:

- use brainstorming to list the driving and restraining forces
- graphically display them (arrows up and arrows down)
- assign numbers to reflect their relative influence on the scores
- agree on one or two forces to concentrate on
- monitor the customer satisfaction scores to measure success

- start over

⌘

FOSBURY FLOP

About every other time a member of the Breakfast Club uses the expression "thinking outside the box," one of our members retells the story of the "Fosbury Flop."

Some background: first, the expression means to be creative and do away with old ways of doing things; second, "Fosbury Flop" refers to the high jump technique in which the jumper goes over the bar headfirst and backward. It is named after Dick Fosbury.

Dick began experimenting with his unique approach when he was sixteen years old. In two years, his best jump improved from a little over five feet to over six feet, six inches!

He went on to win the 1968 Olympic gold medal. In the same year he became the first person ever to jump over seven feet indoors.

Twelve years later, thirteen of the sixteen finalists in the Olympic high jump were using the "Fosbury Flop."

Imagine for how many years coaches throughout the world were teaching young athletes the "right" way to high jump. One sixteen year old changed it all!

So, every time we're darn sure of ourselves, we may want to remember the "Fosbury Flop".

⌘

WATERMELON

"Would anyone like a free watermelon?" asked a Breakfast Club member at the start of last week's meeting.

"Give us the story," responded another member.

"Well, since two of my children are home from college and the third will be a senior in high school, I feel like I'm living in Grand Central Station. I thought it would help me keep track of everyone's goings on and improve communication if I put a message board in the kitchen. I tried it last Wednesday by indicating we needed two watermelons for a family picnic on Saturday. Bad idea! My husband and each of the children ended up buying two melons."

"Yep, just like e-mail messages," added another member. "If you address a request to several co-workers, usually one of two things happens: it doesn't get done because everyone thinks someone else will do it, or everyone does it and time has been wasted."

We agreed it is a good idea to send specific requests to one person and maybe copy others who may be able to help. It's okay to address a call for volunteers to numerous people and then inform all recipients with the names of those who volunteered.

⤎⤏

FRIENDS WELCOME HERE

"My husband got a big kick out of a door knocker he saw at a flea market," said a member as she joined our group. "It was engraved with 'Friends welcome anytime, relatives and co-workers by appointment only.'"

That prompted a number of good-natured, humorous stories about relatives. But one member quickly mentioned that relatives and co-workers can become friends as well.

We agreed that everything goes better with friends. In fact, research shows that people who have friends tend to have better physical health and report a better sense of psychological well-being than those with weak or no network of friends.

Friends provide emotional support, information to help us make decisions, and help with practical needs like baby-sitting in an emergency.

Work friendships often start when a small favor is performed and the favor is returned. Of course, someone must start the chain reaction. That usually happens when a "people person" makes a genuine gesture of assistance. It's then up to the rest of us to respond in kind.

There's no telling where the chain of events could go. A strong friendship may develop. A friend could even become a son-in-law and lose drop-in privileges!

⤎⤏

FUN AT WORK?

"I don't care if you do call me a curmudgeon, I want to see a business case for all this sociability and 'fun at work' stuff," grumbled a staff member as he joined last week's Breakfast Club meeting.

"Listen to this," replied another member as she read from *The Character of a Corporation* by Rob Goffee and Gareth Jones:

> *For the business itself, the benefits of high sociability are many. First, most employees agree that working in such an environment is a pleasure, which promotes high morale and esprit de*

corps. Sociability is also often a boon to creativity because it fosters teamwork, the sharing of information, and openness to new ideas. Healthy sociability also creates an environment in which people are more likely to go beyond the formal requirements of their jobs. They work harder than technically necessary to help their colleagues—that is, their community—look good and succeed.

"Do you think it's worth a try?" continued the reader. "Maybe," was the response as we moved on to another topic.

Business should be fun. Without fun, people are left wearing emotional raincoats most of their working lives. Building fun into business is vital; it brings life into our daily being. Fun is a powerful motive for most of our activities and should be a direct part of our livelihood. We should not relegate it to something we buy after work with money we earn.

- Michael Phillips

᠍᠍᠍

GENERATION X

No doubt you've heard of "baby boomers" and "Generation X." Sociologists and the media define those born between (and including) 1946 and 1964 as "baby boomers." The term Generation X was coined by Douglas Coupland in his 1991 novel, *Generation X: Tales for an Accelerated Culture.* In 1998, Education Week defined Generation X-ers as those born between 1968 and 1979.

Much has been written about the differences between these two groups, especially related to the workplace. Some writers have called Gen X-ers tough to motivate. Yet Gen X-ers describe themselves as caring, committed, and seeking opportunities for learning and leadership.

There is little doubt that managers must manage the two groups differently. In their book *Twenty-Something: Managing & Motivating Today's New Work Force,* Lawrence J. Bradford and Claire Raines identify eight core values of the Generation X employees: they are self-oriented, want "quantity" time, have an extended adolescence, feel disillusioned, are materialistic, want to have fun, are slow to commit, and don't bow to authority.

The book also listed these workplace "turn-ons" and "turn-offs" for Gen X-ers:

Turn-Offs: Hearing about the past; inflexibility about time; workaholism; being watched/scrutinized; feeling disrespected.

Turn-Ons: Recognition; time with you, their manager; learning how what they are doing now is making them more marketable; opportunity to learn new things; fun at work; small, unexpected rewards for a job well done.

We, as managers, must not assume our associates have the same values and views of work as we do, or that they are driven by the same things we are.

⌒⌒⌒

GIVING THANKS

Thanksgiving is the day our country sets aside so we can give thanks for everything we have as individuals and as citizens. At the expense of sounding a bit corny (it's never stopped us in the past), the Breakfast Club sees the Thanksgiving season as a time to give thanks at work, too.

No doubt, supervisors have many good relationships with their team members. And they are constantly building relationships with new team members. Unfortunately, according to a Maritz Poll, about twenty-six percent of employees say their supervisor seldom or never thanks them for a job well done.

So today, as you reflect on your own good fortunes, think about expressing your thanks to those who help you get the job done, day in and day out.

⌒⌒⌒

GOOD BOSS

Some Breakfast Club thoughts on managing others:

- Let employees know how you prefer to addressed. Find out how they prefer to be addressed.
- Praise in public. Criticize in private.
- Share the credit. Most successes result from team effort. If your boss congratulates you, let him know you couldn't have done it without the other members of your team.
- Give employees the tools needed to do the job. Management controls all resources. You wouldn't attempt to repair a car without the correct tools and equipment. Don't expect your employees to accomplish a comparable task without the proper resources.
- Address problems quickly. Ignoring problems or taking weeks or months to address them gives the impression you have little interest in your team's well-being.
- Solicit ideas. Work is complex, and those who are closest to it are

in the best position to offer ideas. Similarly, when you ask someone to do something, give him or her the background and reasons to help them make good decisions.

- Don't play favorites. It undermines morale and team cooperation.
- Keep your staff informed of what is going on in the department, division, and company. Don't let rumors be their only source of information.
- Let workers know how they are doing. You are more than a boss. You are also a coach and teacher. Give them feedback and support to help them improve not only for your team, but also for them personally.

Casey Stengel had this tip, "The secret of managing is to keep the guys who hate you away from the guys who are undecided."

❦

SOUTH

Next time you're having a bad day at the managerial helm, compare your situation to this:

In 1914, Sir Ernest Shackleton led a twenty-seven man crew on an ill-fated expedition to Antarctica. An unusually cold summer caused his ship, HMS Endurance, to get hopelessly stuck in the ice. The ship was crushed and sank in the Weddell Sea 1,200 miles from civilization. The crew walked, drifted on ice floes, sailed in lifeboats over treacherous seas, and climbed mountains to reach help. They lived for months in temperatures that sometimes got so cold they could hear the water freeze. They were perpetually soaked and endured gale force winds. They often had to be on the lookout for predatory sea leopards that could burst through the ice and attack them. But, by all accounts (many diaries and photographs are available), Shackleton was able to maintain high morale. The harrowing experience lasted two years and "Not a life lost and we have been through Hell."

Shackleton's leadership skills have recently begun to attract much attention and study. One admirer said he learned this from Shackleton: "Never give up, don't be afraid to lead, follow your gut, and remember, it's about people."

❦

CUSTOMER SERVICE

"Another bad customer service experience," announced a member as she joined our group. She continued, "For several days I tried unsuccessfully to access part of a company's web site. Out of frustration, I telephoned and told the customer service rep about the problem. The best he could do is tell me he received lots of calls about that. I got the impression he was as frustrated with his employer as I was."

"I had just the opposite experience with one of our hospitals," responded another member. "I used our services and noticed an opportunity for improvement. I wrote a letter to a VP. Not only did I receive a nice response, the situation was improved."

We agreed that a workforce that feels powerless is one of an organization's worst enemies. The organization stagnates, talented people leave it, and customers go elsewhere.

⚭⚭⚭

GRANDPA SAYS…

A member joined the Breakfast Club meeting with this comment: "My daughter asked me 'When Grandpa sees something he really likes he says: "Someone knows what they're doing." What does he mean?'"

I suggested we ask Grandpa. His response: "I guess I mean that someone decided to put forth the extra effort to move from being good at something to being great at it."

The Breakfast Club had a lively discussion about Grandpa's words of wisdom. We agreed that the first step to being great at something is to muster the confidence and courage to really try. It could be sewing, heart surgery, gardening, managing, parenting, or public speaking. The next step is to put forth the never-ending effort to learn and improve.

We also agreed, oddly enough, that fear of success can be as daunting as fear of failure.

> *Any activity becomes creative when the doer cares about doing it right, or better.*
>
> > - John Updike

> *Our doubts are traitors, and make us lose the good we oft might win by fearing attempt.*
>
> > - William Shakespeare

> *People procrastinate because they are afraid of the success that they know will result if they move ahead now. Because success is heavy, carries a responsibility with it, it is much easier to pro-*

crastinate and live on the "someday I'll" philosophy.

- Denis Waitley

❦

GRESHAM'S LAW

A member arrived late for a Breakfast Club meeting. "Sorry, my early morning meeting went long. And to boot, we ran out of time before we got to some important agenda items."

"A variation of Gresham's Law?" asked the team's economics major. Our blank stares prompted this explanation: "Gresham's Law states that bad money drives out good money. In meetings, less important topics can easily run long and drive out important topics."

We agreed that managing a meeting and tactfully keeping attendees on track is very difficult. We also agreed that a prioritized agenda distributed before a meeting can be a big help.

P.S.: The Breakfast Club members were forced to practice what we preach. After fifteen minutes of a lecture on Gresham's Law, we "politely" yawned in unison to close the topic.

❦

GROUP DYNAMICS

The Super Bowl got the Breakfast Club talking about the similarities between sports and business. As talk turned to motivation, the name Lou Holtz came up. Coach Holtz was credited with revitalizing the Notre Dame Football program some years ago and bringing success to many other programs during his coaching career. He is considered by many to be a master of motivational speaking. He suggests that any group is likely to succeed if everyone involved can say this about everyone else in the group:

1. I can trust you.
2. You are committed to excellence.
3. You care about me.

Agree?

❦

GUESTOLOGY

According to the *Disney Approach to Quality Service for Healthcare Profes-*

sionals, organizations must clearly understand patients and customers in order to exceed their service expectations.

We must identify:

- What customers **need** from us in order to have a satisfying experience.
- What customers **want** from us.
- The stereotypes customers have of our organization and industry—positive and negative. We must reinforce the positive stereotypes and dispel the negative ones.
- The emotions the customers experience while in our organization or communicating with it. All associates must understand the emotional needs of patients and family members and have the skills to effectively deal with those emotions.

∽≈∾

GUILTY!

"I think I need to attend a class on dealing with feelings of guilt," announced a member at the start of last week's meeting.

"Give us the story," sighed another member.

"Our lawn, which hasn't required mowing for a month, finally needed it. On Saturday morning I asked my seventeen-year-old son to cut it. We were expecting guests at about five o'clock, and I wanted it done by then. By three o'clock he hadn't started, and I noticed him backing the car out of the driveway. I ran up to the car and, in a not too friendly voice, asked, "Where do you think you're going?"

"To get gasoline to cut the lawn," he replied.

"Lack of feedback causes problems at home and work," volunteered another member. She went on to say it might have helped if Mom suggested that the lawn be mowed by four o'clock. It would have helped if the son told his Mom he was about to mow the lawn but needed gasoline.

At work, simple messages like "I've started on the project," or "I expect to have it done by noon tomorrow," or "I'm struggling and am afraid I may not make the deadline" go a long way to avoiding confusion—and guilt.

∽≈∾

HERZBERG'S THEORY

Every manager longs for highly motivated team members. Social scientists and managers alike have long debated exactly what motivates us at work.

Frederick Herzberg, a contemporary of Abraham Maslow, proposed a theory about job factors that motivate employees. He divided work life into motivators (satisfiers) and hygiene factors (dissatisfiers).

Satisfiers motivate us. Dissatisfiers do not motivate us (but their absence can create job dissatisfaction). Improvements to satisfiers are likely to produce long-term positive effects in job performance. Improvements to dissatisfiers produce only short-term improvements in job attitudes and performance, which quickly fall back to previous levels.

Now for a quiz. According to Herzberg, each of the following is either a satisfier or a dissatisfier:

- achievement
- advancement
- company policies
- interpersonal relations
- recognition
- responsibility
- salary
- supervision
- the work itself
- working conditions

∽∾

Satisfiers and Dissatisfiers

Here are the answers to the quiz on Frederick Herzberg's work satisfiers and dissatisfiers:

Motivators/Satisfiers (Long-Term)	Hygiene Factors/Dissatisfiers (Short-Term)
Achievement	Company Policies
Advancement	Interpersonal Relations
Recognition	Salary
Responsibility	Supervision
The Work Itself	Working Conditions

Any surprises?

∽∾

Hidden Talents

"I'm all for the talent show provided no one here hopes to sing," remarked our kidder as he joined our meeting.

"I beg your pardon," replied a member. "I paid my way through college by singing in a rock band."

It turned out none of us knew that about her. And as the conversation continued, we learned a lot about each other's hidden talents and interests.

We agreed that busy managers often forget that a person is not the job. Everyone has talents, skills, and interests that transcend their current position. Skilled managers get to know their colleagues. That way they can tap the talents and also help associates develop.

> *Every person I work with knows something better than me. My job is to listen long enough to find it and use it.*
> - Jack Nichols

❧❧❧

HINDSIGHT

"So close yet so far," announced a Breakfast Club member as he joined our last meeting.

"Please confess," suggested another member.

"I was part of the team that developed the process to obtain and track over 13,000 signatures on the Confidentiality and Data Security Agreement Form. Just about the time we were congratulating ourselves on our clever use of personalized forms and window envelopes, problems arose."

He went on to describe two kinks in the process. First, most of the returned envelopes were sealed. Opening them added an unexpected step to the process. Second, team members were unaware that some departments had distributed forms in advance of the mass mailing. That meant some associates signed and returned two forms.

In our informal After Action Review we identified two opportunities for improvement. First, we could have better communicated that a mass mailing was planned. Second, a test mailing would have uncovered the fact that the envelopes would be returned sealed. We could then have tested other approaches.

We agreed that it is healthy for people, departments, and organizations to admit their mistakes and learn from them.

❧❧❧

I Botched It Up

"I botched it up," announced the newest and youngest member of the Breakfast Club as he joined our meeting.

"Please confess," suggested the senior member.

"Three of my team members came to me with a problem. Because I'm a new manager, I felt compelled to appear confident and decisive and I quickly offered a solution. They came back three days later to announce my decision caused unexpected results that made things much worse."

Everyone in the group smiled. It seemed we all had made similar mistakes early in our careers.

"Just as managers can use the 'dump and run' approach to delegation, team members can use the 'dump it on the manager's door step' approach to problems," added an experienced member.

We agreed most processes are complex, and it is unrealistic to expect any one person, even if she is the manager, to know everything about them. We decided managers must make it clear that problems are to be accompanied by a few possible courses of action that can be discussed.

Such an approach produces better solutions. It also is another way in which managers can express respect and confidence in all the team members.

❧

Improve Your Talent

The Breakfast Club discussed New Year's resolutions during our first annual holiday party. Naturally, the conversation drifted toward our roles as managers.

This question was brought up (we're really a wild bunch): Should managers encourage associates (and themselves) to improve on work-related weaknesses or fine-tune their strengths?

The initial response from most was "improve on weaknesses." After all, we reasoned, that's where the most improvement is needed and where the gains can be greatest.

One clever member used the Socratic Method to challenge our thinking. "Is it fair to liken a work team to a football team?" she asked.

"Good analogy," we replied.

"Does a football coach prefer the quarterback to practice becoming a better passer or better blocker?"

"Passer," was the unanimous response.

"Does the football coach prefer the kicker to work at becoming a better kicker or better passer?" was the next question.

"Kicker," we said in unison.

It began to sink in. Teams are at their best when all persons are in a position befitting their talents and skills. Perhaps asking the naturally disorganized person to become more organized is like asking the quarterback to become the punter. Perhaps asking the naturally quiet associate to become a "people" person is like asking the place kicker to become a fullback.

"But that doesn't mean we shouldn't expect associates to improve specific behavior," elaborated our philosopher. Asking everyone to report to work on time is reasonable. Asking everyone to be gregarious is probably futile.

Perhaps Stephen R. Covey said it best: "Strength lies in differences, not in similarities."

⌒⌒⌒

IMPROVING ON TALENT

"I enjoyed watching Marcus Buckingham and George Schaefer on TV last week," announced a member as she joined our meeting.

"Salient points please," requested our taciturn member.

Here is her summary:

The chief responsibility of a manager is to turn a person's talent into performance. Marcus states that each person's greatest room for growth is in the area of his greatest strength. We agreed that talents cry out to be used and using them is rewarding in its own right. Great managers work with people to help them understand their strengths, improve them, and bolster their confidence to use them.

The chief responsibility of a leader is to rally people to a better future. We agreed that the future is a scary place. The leader who clearly communicates where she wants to take us helps build our confidence and reduces our anxiety.

⌒⌒⌒

INERTIA

A few meetings ago the Breakfast Club members discussed inertia—of the management kind. We wondered why it is so tempting, and common, to delay action. We stare at problems and do nothing as if the problems will go away if we simply wait long enough. Of course, they seldom go away and quite often get worse.

We asked our intern to look into it. She presented this paragraph from

F. Scott Peck's book *The Road Less Traveled*:

> *This inclination to ignore problems is once again a simple manifestation of an unwillingness to delay gratification. Confronting problems is, as I have said, painful. To willingly confront a problem early, before we are forced to confront it by circumstances, means to put aside something pleasant or less painful for something more painful. It is choosing to suffer now in the hope of future gratification rather than choosing to continue present gratification in the hope that future suffering will not be necessary.*

❧

GREAT EXPLANATION. IS IT OBVIOUS?

One of the Breakfast Club members arrived at the last meeting in an upbeat mood. "Several months ago I was struggling with staffing issues and asked my team when we were busiest. 'On Mondays,' they replied confidently and in unison. When I asked them how they knew, they said it was simply obvious. After much discussion, I convinced them to keep a log."

"It turned out Wednesdays were consistently the busiest by a significant margin. Everyone was shocked. We concluded it's hard to get into the swing of things on Mondays, and it just seemed that there was more activity than there really was. We got a laugh out of it and learned a lesson at the same time."

The Breakfast Club agreed that good data helps in making good decisions. We also agreed with C. West Churchman's comment that "It's always wise to raise questions about the most obvious and simple assumptions."

❧

IT PAYS TO PAY ATTENTION

First, some background for our younger readers: long before CDs and the iPod, music came on records. In the early 1900s, records were played on a hand-cranked phonograph that used needles to play the music as the record rotated. The needles wore out very, very quickly.

In 1914, the ship *Endurance* set sail for an expedition to Antarctica. Because the trip was expected to last well over a year, they brought records for entertainment. They also ordered 5,000 needles.

Imagine their disappointment when, on the high seas, they tried to play a record only to discover they had a box of five thousand sewing needles!

We're told they left out the C in the Plan Do Check Act cycle.

∽≈∽

It's All In The Delivery...

Opening day isn't far off, so some of the Breakfast Club members have begun debating the ideal batting order. Some claim it is crucial to success, and others say data indicates otherwise.

A member used the debate to educate us on some interesting research.

Briefly, a group of volunteers from Yale University School of Management were brought together to act the part of managers faced with a problem that required much cooperation.

They did not know the meetings included a conspirator. This trained actor always spoke first and always made identical arguments. But he did it in different emotional keys:

- cheerful, ebullient enthusiasm
- relaxed, serene warmth
- depressed sluggishness
- unpleasant and hostile irritability

As you can guess, researchers wanted to determine if he could infect the group with his emotional state, like spreading a virus among unknowing victims.

The emotions did spread like a virus. Just as important, objective measures showed the groups were more effective when he led off with enthusiasm and warmth.

At work, at play, or at home, emotional undercurrents are always present. Perhaps they play a bigger role than we realize?

∽≈∽

It's All In The Timing...

"No good deed goes unpunished," announced a member as he joined our meeting. "I decided to be a thoughtful father and compliment my fourteen-year-old daughter. So, I said something nice about her new blouse. She groaned and remarked this was the third time I've seen her in it."

Another member recounted saying something nice about the new kitchen curtains only to be told they've been there two weeks.

We agreed it is easy to become blind to the things and people that surround us. We decided it is especially easy to take for granted the many good qualities of our work team members. We left the meeting intent on not only seeing those good qualities but paying timely compliments as well.

We are the most impressionable creatures on God's green earth, and a kind word can set us up for a whole week.
                                                      - Sydney J. Harris

Some people pay a compliment as if they expected a receipt.
                                                      - Kin Hubbard

It's Not The Method

One of our Breakfast Club members has a strong interest in primary education. Before our last meeting, she read this to us:

"It is amazing to see so many different pedagogical approaches, often at odds with each other, succeed in instilling children with a sense of intellectual curiosity and discipline. Apparently what counts is not so much the method used, but the teacher's enthusiasm and concern for each student as an individual."

We concluded that these are also the basic ingredients of good management.

P.S.: The quote is from *The Evolving Self* by Mihaly Csikszentmihalyi.

It's Rather Timely

Here is a summary of our thoughts about e-mail and voice mail etiquette.

- If you will be unavailable to answer voice mail or e-mail, leave a message to that effect.
- Respond to mail within twenty-four hours. (Some members suggest a quicker response but twenty-four hours was common.)
- The "To" block in e-mail should contain the name of the person responsible for acting on information in the message or from whom you expect a response. In other words, unless the recipient is expected to do something as a result of receiving the mail, don't put his/her name on the "To" line.

- If you're the only person on the "To" line, it is understood if actions are required, you'll do it. If you'll do it, there is probably no need to say that.
- If you cannot do it, quickly say so. E-mail to say "I received your message and hope to have your information by ..."
- If you don't have the time to engage people in conversation, simply use the "reply by voice mail" function on the phone. A short message to say that you are working on their request and will call later saves a lot of "follow-up" time by the requestor.
- Make the subject line meaningful and succinct. This helps when the reader needs to find and/or refer back to messages at a later date. A subject line of "Help" is of little value.
- When responding to e-mail, include the original message to provide a reminder.
- As much as possible, keep to a single topic in each e-mail.
- Typing in upper case is the equivalent of shouting. DON'T SHOUT. However, a short stretch of all uppercase can be used to emphasize a point.
- Do not send e-mail when feeling a strong negative emotion. Use the draft feature of e-mail and revise the message after you have calmed down.
- Remember that e-mail is not private; employers have the right to look at all employee e-mail sent through a company computer.

✂✁✄

JOB SATISFACTION

One of the Breakfast Club interns asked if the senior members had any advice on job satisfaction. "Glad you asked," replied a member as she opened her planner. "I read this a few years ago and have carried it with me ever since.

"My advice is to go into something and stay with it until you like it. You can't like it until you obtain expertise in that work. And once you are an expert, it's a pleasure."

Those words were spoken by Milton Garland who, at the age of one hundred two, was America's oldest known wage earner. He had worked for the same firm for seventy-eight years. He gave his advice at Washington's National Press Club, which is headquartered in a building where Mr. Garland helped install the refrigeration equipment in the late 1920s. At the time of the interview, he was working twenty hours per week coordinating his employer's international patents and training young workers.

Although not every staff member agreed with Mr. Garland's philosophy, we did agree that it helps to keep an open mind about one's profession, company, job, and team members. Don't jump ship before giving them a fair chance.

If you have a job without aggravations, you don't have a job.
- Malcolm Forbes

◌◠◠◠◌

JUDGE YOURSELF FIRST

At last week's Breakfast Club meeting, a member read a few paragraphs from a book. It hit a bit too close to home for some of us. Here it is:

"Most managers, when they view their group, are supervising, judging, and ranking performance of the individual workers. But a leader judges his own performance when he observes his group. In his mind he is determining what he has to emphasize or de-emphasize, what action he has to take to foster improvement.

"He must see that those in need of special help get it. If they need additional training, he must see they receive it. If they are beyond being helped by additional training, he must see that they are moved to positions where they can contribute and make sure they are properly trained."

P.S.: This can be found in the book *Dr. Deming: The American Who Taught the Japanese About Quality* by Rafael Aguayo.

◌◠◠◠◌

JUST LISTEN!

"I just returned from a meeting in which, to use the vernacular, a participant was 'talking crazy,'" announced a member as he joined us.

We commiserated with stories of our own. When the laughter died down a member asked, "Did you try temporarily dropping your ingrained point of view and listen?"

A lively discussion followed. We agreed that it is common to immediately prepare a comeback, or wonder why someone would hold such a bizarre point of view, or interrupt the speaker, or simply zone out. We also agreed it is wise to actually concentrate on the speaker's message rather than our own automatic retort.

It is a curious fact that of all the illusions that beset mankind none is quite so curious as that tendency to suppose that we are mentally and morally superior to those who differ from us in opinion.

- Elbert Hubbard

༓

TWO WAY COMMUNICATION

A few articles ago we wrote about using e-mail to request information. A member shared this tip with us:

> *One of the communication tools that I have found to be valuable is to acknowledge an e-mail with estimates of when the request can be fulfilled or a status update when the request has been fulfilled. Recently, I received a request that would require some considerable research. Rather than just beginning the task, I responded to the requester as soon as I got the e-mail saying, "Just wanted you to know I am working on this request and expect to have something for you by tomorrow." A simple estimate of time helps the person on the other end know what to expect. Or, if I am asked to put through forms or messages I will try to send an e-mail saying, "I have sent your form on through to (whoever) for processing." I think this kind of simple follow-up can sometimes prevent a more lengthy follow-up later.*

We agree.

༓

KNOWLEDGE EQUALS ACTION - MAYBE

"How did your son do in last night's tennis match?" asked a member as we waited for the meeting to begin.

"You know he was very nervous. He had never seen his opponent play but spoke to him last week. My son was impressed with his confidence and knowledge of the game. But his coach said not to worry because his opponent simply 'talked a good game.'"

That brought up the fascinating book *The Knowing Doing Gap: How Smart Companies Turn Knowledge Into Action* by Jeffrey Pfeffer and Robert Sutton. The book addresses this conundrum: people and organizations often know what to do, but don't do it.

The authors offer well-researched, intriguing reasons. Here's one we found particularly interesting:

"Unfortunately for getting anything done in organizations, one of the best ways of sounding smart is to be critical of others' ideas.

"But, at the end of the day, something still needs to get done. If all that has happened is that those with the courage to actually propose something have been devastated in the process, the organization will be filled with clever put-down artists and with inactivity. This situation arises because the people are so clever, and so determined to appear clever, that they will succeed at critiquing everything to death."

> *Nothing will ever be attempted if all possible objections must first be overcome.*
> - Samuel Johnson

❧

LEAD ON

In a previous article we touched on leadership. There may be a tendency to think of leaders as only those at the very top of an organization. Not true.

Our associates are leaders inside and outside the hospitals. We have formal and informal leaders in organizations such as churches, clubs, civic organizations, political parties, and athletic organizations. And we bring leadership talents to work with us.

In fact, a truly vibrant organization looks to every associate to lead. And we do that when we:

- Contribute in team meetings
- Respect differing points of view
- Show new associates "the ropes"
- Suggest ways to improve processes
- Demonstrate integrity by doing what we say we are going to do
- Tactfully challenge the status quo
- Nip gossip in the bud
- Praise good work
- Be a team player by helping co-workers who may be struggling
- Alert the boss when he or she may be about to make a mistake
- Be a good follower
- Help keep a meeting on track
- Support the boss in a difficult, controversial decision
- Accept change and help implement it
- Expect excellence from ourselves and others
- Lead On…

Leadership is not magnetic personality–that can just as well be a glib tongue. It is not making friends and influencing people–that is flattery. Leadership is lifting a person's vision to higher sights, the raising of a person's performance to a higher standard, the building of a personality beyond its normal limitations.

- Peter F. Drucker

❦

LESSONS LEARNED

Every day throughout organizations, work teams complete projects, events, major undertakings, and solve a crisis or two. Here's an approach to what some call an "After Action Review" and others call "Lessons Learned."

Ask these four questions and document the answers for future reference:

1. What was the plan?
2. What actually happened?
   What worked well?
   What didn't work so well?
3. Why did it happen the way it did?
4. What should we do to improve?

Avoid the temptation to concentrate exclusively on what went wrong. In fact, the secret to a meaningful "Lessons Learned" session is to emphasize the good and the bad. Starting with a detailed description of the many things that went right builds team spirit and confidence. It helps generate the willingness and determination to improve on weaknesses.

A previous article mentioned that "dream teams" celebrate successes. Celebrating successes—both small and large—is another way to end projects on a positive note. It helps break work into manageable segments, lifts spirits, and gives the team something to look forward to.

❦

LET THE GOOD TIMES ROLL

"Men!" announced a female member as she entered the room for the Breakfast Club meeting.

"Let us have it," replied a male member with a knowing smile.

"My twenty-two-year-old son has been in his first real job for just five months. Now that he has a steady pay check, he went into debt to buy an expensive sports car."

"Just as C. Northcote Parkinson observed," replied another member.

A stimulating discussion followed. We agreed that it is difficult for individuals, families, companies, and governments to be frugal during financially good times. But we also agreed that it is just as important to watch our pennies during good times as during tough times. If we don't, the good times simply evaporate into tough times.

Later in this book we describe Parkinson's observation.

∾

LET'S TALK

Our email system has recently been upgraded on many of our computers. That prompted the Breakfast Club members to discuss the interesting ways email continues to change the way we communicate at work and at home. Anyone with teenagers is familiar with instant messaging and text messaging.

We again asked our intern to do some research. He returned with a summary that did not surprise us. Although email is fast and easy, it probably is not the best tool to use to inspire your helpers.

As Howard Friedman, a psychologist at the University of California at Irvine, observes, "The essence of eloquent, passionate, spirited communication seems to involve the use of facial expressions, voices, gestures, and body movements to transmit emotions."

We concluded that email is a good vehicle to communicate facts, but high energy, face-to-face communication is the best way to make good things happen.

∾

LISTEN UP

In a previous Breakfast Club meeting, we kicked around Mike Abrashoff's suggestion to listen aggressively. All of us had read and heard lots about good listening. We challenged ourselves to come up with just three basic principles. Here they are:

Ignore rank. Good ideas are not the sole purview of highly experienced workers, executives, or professionals. If our level of attention is tied to those factors, we're likely to miss out on useful ideas. Worse, we could discourage others from sharing their ideas with us.

Just listen. Wondering about how you'll respond is putting the cart before the horse. You'll likely "hear" better if you don't worry about how you'll respond.

Pause. Don't feel obligated to respond quickly. Pausing a moment before responding is a sign of respect. It could also prevent the wrong words from escaping.

> *Everything has been said before, but since nobody listens we have to keep going back and beginning all over again.*
>
> — Andre Gide

✧

SATISFACTION EQUALS PROFITABILITY

In the business world, the long-standing yardstick used to measure performance has been almost exclusively profitability. Businesses simply looked at the bottom line to determine how well they were doing. Although profit will always be the ultimate measure of business survivability, other factors are getting increasingly more attention. Customer and employee satisfaction are closely measured because they greatly influence profitability.

Tight labor markets for specific jobs make employee retention more important than ever. So, employers are interested in becoming the "employer of choice" in their geographical area. They work hard at developing a good reputation so they can more easily recruit and retain the best and brightest employees who will help the company prosper.

It's an interesting twist of fate. Our robust, knowledge-based economy has quickly made employers acutely aware that employees are the engines that move the business. The new equation is: satisfied employees make satisfied customers who cause the profit. Sounds like the perfect win-win situation, doesn't it?

✧

LUMBERJACK'S BALL

Last Saturday the Breakfast Club held its annual Lumberjack party. It's a lot like Super Bowl and Kentucky Derby parties. We sit around the big-screen TV and cheer as competitors chop and saw huge logs.

And, like most of our parties, the conversation drifted to the age-old question, which contributes most to an organization's success: people or systems?

Those in the "people" camp argue that talented, creative, dedicated, loyal people make organizations successful.

Those in the "system" camp argue that talented people entangled in terribly poor systems will become frustrated and leave the organization. Others may give up trying to improve things and simply go through the motions. "It's like giving a very dull axe *with a cracked handle* to an experienced lumberjack," summarizes one Breakfast Club member.

⤜⤛

MAKE YOUR TEAM A "HOWLING" SUCCESS

"My son's Boy Scout troop visited Wolf Park over the weekend," announced a member as he joined our meeting. "I think wolves can teach us a few things," he continued.

"Tell us more," suggested another member.

"One of the reasons wolves howl is to stay in contact with each other over long distances. Separate a wolf from its pack, and very soon it will begin howling. And each wolf's howl is unique and allows wolves to identify each other."

"So, what's to learn?" asked our resident skeptic.

"Well, since they communicate often and well, it seems there are few surprises among wolves. They know one another's whereabouts and activities."

We agreed that members of organizations often fail to communicate important information to others. We become wrapped up in a project, problem, or crisis and forget that others in the organization may need to know about it.

We agreed we often just don't howl enough.

P.S.: There really is a Wolf Park and it is located in Lafayette, Indiana. It's a wildlife education and research facility open to the public and home to wolves, foxes, coyotes, and bison.

⤜⤛

MANAGEMENT IS AN ART

The Breakfast Club members enjoyed these wise words from Edgar Schein:

> *The most important idea that has stood the test of time is that management is not a profession in the sense of having a discrete body of knowledge and skills: it is an art. And so improvisational skills are far more important than any rules or*

formulas.

Studies of variations in organizational cultures between industries and countries make it perfectly obvious that the management process is different in different places. Even something as general as management by objectives doesn't hold everywhere. I think the ability to improvise and quickly feel what the situation needs are the most important skills a manager needs to have.

Edgar Schein is an expert on industrial and organizational psychology. He joined the faculty of the Sloan School at the Massachusetts Institute of Technology (1956) and established a private consultancy to government and industry. His books include *Organizational Culture and Leadership* (1985).

꙾꙾꙾

MANAGER'S REFERENCE GUIDE
Studies in *The Desk Manager's Reference* indicate that ninety-nine percent of all employees are motivated by some combination of the needs for:

- Achievement: succeed at their jobs
- Power: to be in control of processes they are accountable for
- Affiliation: enjoy interacting with others
- Autonomy: be independent
- Esteem: receive praise (but don't overdo it)
- Safety and Security: to know they will have a job tomorrow
- Equity: treated fairly

The more a manager knows about what motivates her helpers, the better she is able to improve the work environment for everyone—worker, customer, manager.

꙾꙾꙾

MANAGING EXPECTATIONS
"The twin boys who live next door to me are almost seventeen years old. I suspect they are a bit more rebellious than average," mentioned a member as we waited for our meeting to begin.

"They could almost be considered out of control," she continued.

It turns out the boys' father is a strict disciplinarian who raised them in an atmosphere of punishment and threats of punishment. As could be predicted, the father got his desired effect while the boys were young. His approach no longer works on teenagers.

We agreed that fear as a management style also only works for the short term. It destroys initiative and creativity. It also encourages talented people whose skills are in demand to seek work elsewhere. And it certainly doesn't make for a great place to work.

✐

Mary, Mary...

"Say, how come you're not sharing vegetables from your garden this year?" asked a member as our amateur farmer joined our meeting.

"Entropy," was the reply.

Our blank looks were cue enough for a more elaborate answer.

He went on to say that entropy is "the inevitable and steady deterioration of a system or society." It seems that he spent many of his summer evenings and weekends working on a retaining wall in the front of his house. He ignored his vegetable garden and the weeds took over.

His story prompted a stimulating conversation. We concluded that all human activities suffer from entropy: friendships, organizational processes, family relationships, lawns, work relationships, and gardens.

In short, if we don't spend time nurturing them, they inevitably deteriorate.

✐

Meetings, Meetings, Meetings

"Are you lugging around another John Kenneth Galbraith book?" asked one of the members at last week's Breakfast Club meeting.

"Sure, and listen to this quote by Mr. Galbraith," replied the bibliophile. "Meetings are indispensable when you don't want to do anything."

We spent the meeting talking about meetings. We agreed they could be the bane of managers. We also came up with these reasons why:

- No clear purpose or agenda
- People coming late and leaving early
- The same people dominate
- Predictably boring and humorless
- Participation is not encouraged
- "Groundhog Day Movie" syndrome: covering the same topics over and over

- Drifting off topic
- No clear decisions or assignments
- Jumping up and down to respond to or make phone calls

***

MEMORABLE EVENT

At our last meeting a member mentioned her daughter's high school class discussed the poem "Incident" by Countee Cullen that ends with:

> I saw the whole of Baltimore
> From May until December;
> Of all the things that happened there
> That's all that I remember.

We agreed that our experiences, especially hospital visits, can be greatly colored by a single experience. A perfectly good three-day stay can be ruined by a single event. Some call this the law of the memorable event. The memorable event is the story that we, as patients, tell over and over again to anyone who will listen.

These stories can become our image with the public.

It may seem unfair that single, even simple, events can be so influential. We agreed that attention to every detail is what separates the great from the good organization.

***

THERE'S A MOOSE ON THE TABLE

A slight difference of opinion arose in our last Breakfast Club meeting. One member announced, "I'd like to put the moose on the table."

She responded to our perplexed looks with a short explanation. Randall Tobias led the pharmaceutical giant Eli Lilly through some difficult times. In his book he says that integrity is usually defined in terms of honesty: don't lie, steal, cheat, or break the law. But he expanded honesty to mean if two people have differing points of view they should confront each other and "put the moose on the table."

That's where tact and sincerity and openness and patience and similar approaches come into play.

P.S." As you can guess, Randall Tobias titled his book *Put the Moose on the Table*.

***

More Meeting Ideas

We received several additional comments about the meeting in which we discussed managing meetings. One member suggested "having a 'parking lot' to put new issues that arise is helpful in keeping the group on task. Those issues can be postponed for future meetings."

The "parking lot" is often a white board or paper on which important topics not germane to the current discussion are recorded for future attention.

P.S.: A member correctly identified managing e-mail (and voicemail and faxes) as another reason that ranks high in making us feel unproductive at work.

⌒⌒

More on Leadership

This is what Warren Bennis has to say about managers and leaders:

- The manager administers; the leader innovates.
- The manager is a copy; the leader is an original.
- The manager maintains; the leader develops.
- The manager focuses on systems and structure; the leader focuses on people.
- The manager relies on control; the leader inspires trust.
- The manager has a short-range view; the leader has a long-range perspective.
- The manager asks how and when; the leader asks what and why.
- The manager has his eye always on the bottom line; the leader has his eye on the horizon.
- The manager imitates; the leader originates.
- The manager accepts the status quo; the leader challenges it.
- The manager is the classic good soldier; the leader is his own person.
- The manager does things right; the leader does the right thing.

P.S.: Warren Bennis was the president of the University of Cincinnati from 1971 to 1977. He developed behaviorist-based management theories in his numerous books on leadership and organizational development and change. He is well known as a consultant to major corporations. His thoughts are from his book *On Becoming a Leader*.

⌒⌒

MOTIVATION

The Breakfast Club members recently asked themselves "How can managers truly motivate their associates?" After a lengthy discussion, we almost concluded they can't!

After all, we reasoned, real motivation comes from within. After further discussion, we agreed managers can, and must, create the conditions under which associates willingly help the department and themselves thrive and grow.

So, what are those conditions? We condensed our ideas to this list:

- Members understand the organization's and department's purpose and goals, and they are compatible with their own.
- Members feel their work is important.
- The team has the resources and training to get the job done.
- The team works together to determine how best to attain goals.
- Associates' talents, skills, and interests match their duties.
- Expectations are clear.
- Members trust one another.
- Everyone (including the manager) gets frequent feedback so they know how they are doing.
- The work atmosphere includes fun and laughter and rewarding relationships.

∽∽∽

MY BUCKET'S GOT A HOLE IN IT...

"Topic for debate," announced our resident troublemaker as he joined our meeting.

He then read this from the book *How Full is Your Bucket?*:

> *Whether we have a long conversation with a friend or simply place an order at a restaurant, every interaction makes a difference. The results of our encounters are rarely neutral; they are almost always positive or negative. And although we take these interactions for granted, they accumulate and profoundly affect our lives.*

We spent the meeting discussing the book. We also kicked around thoughts about what makes for a positive interaction between co-workers. What would you include in the list?

≈≈≈

No Easy Victories

One of our Breakfast Club members suggested we read Dr. Gardner's book, *No Easy Victories*. We did. Here are a few excerpts we found particularly thought provoking:

"Total absence of problems would be the beginning of death for a society or an individual. We aren't constructed to live in that kind of world. We are problem-solvers by nature—problem-seekers, problem-requirers."

"Take the statistical view of rascals and fools. There are so many per thousand in the population. You have to meet your share. If you seem to be meeting more than your share, lie down: you may be tired."

"When events push a fellow worker momentarily off balance, when anxiety and fatigue undermine his judgment, don't punish him for his errors. Restore him."

"What could be more satisfying than to be engaged in work in which every capacity or talent one may have is needed, every lesson one may have learned is used, every value one cares about is furthered?"

P.S.: John Gardner was Secretary of Health, Education, and Welfare (1965–1968). He has served presidents, advised government agencies, founded volunteer organizations, and served on boards and councils of corporations and nonprofit institutions. In 1964, Dr. Gardner was awarded the Presidential Medal of Freedom, the highest civil honor in the United States.

≈≈≈

Off With Their Heads

"Story time," announced a member as he joined our meeting. "I enjoy gardening, and my teenage daughter has recently shown an interest in the hobby. For Father's Day, she gave me several hanging baskets teeming with beautiful petunias. She even volunteered to tend them for me."

"I told her that removing the old blooms would prompt new flowers to quickly come back in great abundance."

"I was disappointed to see the plants doing so poorly. My daughter assured me she was watering, fertilizing, and removing the old blooms. I suggested we go on the porch and take a look. She asked if she should bring a pair of scissors."

"It turns out that she was cutting the blooms off at the stem instead of simply pulling the dead flowers off."

The Breakfast Club members agreed that it is all too easy to assume others know everything we know. We also agreed it's better to over-communicate at the front end of a task than to spend time fixing errors at the other end.

❦

ONLY THE BEST WILL DO

"I saw you pull into the parking lot this morning and was surprised to see you still aren't driving a new car," said one of our members to another while waiting for our meeting to get started.

"Four months ago we started the hunt for the perfect car. I think we have visited every dealer in the Tri-State area—still no new car," was the response.

That prompted a discussion about decision-making. Several of us were of the "absolute best" mentality. We tend to spend much time researching, pondering, analyzing, and discussing before deciding.

Others described settling on merely an "excellent" option. They believe trying to make the absolute best decision is stressful, time-consuming, and often leads to "analysis paralysis," or buyer's remorse.

We all related to the hiring process. In our attempt to find the absolutely ideal candidate, we feel compelled to interview numerous candidates. But in today's labor market if we take too long to decide, the excellent—but not perfect—candidate accepts a position elsewhere and our search starts all over.

We agreed the "absolute best" approach is ultimately impractical because rarely does life or business hold forth the perfect option.

> *Indecision is debilitating; it feeds upon itself; it is, one might almost say, habit-forming. Not only that, but it is contagious; it transmits itself to others.*
>
> - H. A. Hopf

❦

PDCA

A breakfast Club member directed us to a Dartmouth Medical School's Web Site. The following is taken from their *Clinician's Black Bag of Quality Improvement Tools*:

Plan: a change or a test, aimed at improvement.

In this phase, analyze what you intend to improve, looking for areas that hold opportunities for change. The first step is to choose areas that offer the most return for the effort you put in; the biggest bang for your buck. To identify these areas for change, consider using a Flow chart or Pareto chart.

Do: Carry out the change or test (preferably on a small scale). Implement the change you decided on in the plan phase.

Check or Study: the results. What was learned? What went wrong?

This is a crucial step in the PDCA cycle. After you have implemented the change for a short time, you must determine how well it is working. Is it really leading to improvement in the way you had hoped? You must decide on several measures with which you can monitor the level of improvement. Run Charts can be helpful with this measurement.

Act: Adopt the change, abandon it, or run through the cycle again.

After planning a change, implementing and then monitoring it, you must decide whether it is worth continuing that particular change. If it consumed too much of your time, was difficult to adhere to, or even led to no improvement, you may consider aborting the change and planning a new one. However, if the change led to a desirable improvement or outcome, you may consider expanding the trial to a different area, or slightly increasing your complexity. This sends you back into the Plan phase and can be the beginning of the ramp of improvement.

✦

PERFORMANCE REVIEW

No doubt, performance review time is most managers' favorite time of year.

The Breakfast Club looks forward to it just as much as you do. We've come up with a short list of reminders:

- Give this process the attention it deserves.
- Keep in mind you are reviewing work results, not judging a person.
- Gather information so you can compare an associate's work plan with actual accomplishments.
- Consider seeking the opinions of others to get more than just your perspective.
- Review the entire time frame, not just the last few weeks.
- Choose a time when you and your associate will be able to concentrate.
- Set an appointment well in advance of the meeting.
- Don't break your appointment with the associate.

- Ensure privacy.
- Try to sit face to face without a desk between you.
- Open the meeting by stating its purpose.
- Set a tone of openness.
- Concentrate on important issues and don't drift into minutiae.
- Limit the number of things you'd like the associate to try to improve.
- Set objectives for the next review period.
- Sign the forms.
- Shake hands and thank the associate.

⌘

PLEASANTVILLE

In times of sudden and unexpected change, someone is sure to say something like "Who wants to run away to Tahiti?"

The last time a Breakfast Club member said that, the conversation turned to the movie Pleasantville. We won't spoil it for those who haven't seen it, but the film contrasts a town where nothing changes and everything is perfect to the real world. It's sometimes tempting to fantasize about living in the unchanging world of Pleasantville or Mayberry. But the movie reminds us that change is natural and inevitable. It also helps us to open our eyes to the underlying beauty of the complexity, uncertainty, challenges, and even chaos that often come with change. We recommend the film to anyone in health care.

⌘

PRACTICE

"I had an a-ha last night while watching my daughter's basketball team practice," announced a member as she joined our meeting. "Her team practices four hours for every hour of game time. The coach reminds the players that games simply let them know how well they've done in practice."

"It occurred to me that athletes, actors, police officers, and even the military make practice a part of their lives. But managers seldom, if ever, get to practice our art. It seems like we're always in the 'management game' but are seldom coached, rarely practice, and get little feedback from our colleagues."

"Not only that," replied another member "but management rules are not as clear as many other rules in life, and there are no referees. Imagine a 'management referee' blowing a whistle in the middle of a meeting with a 'you're dominating the meeting' foul, or a 'failure to recognize good performance' violation."

We agreed that management courses, training programs, and management articles are the equivalent of practice. If we don't avail ourselves of them we're playing but probably not improving very much.

～☜～

PUT A PLUG IN IT!

A Breakfast Club member emailed this to us:

A woman is standing on the shore of a large lake pondering Continuous Quality Improvement. She notices a man in a rowboat. He's rowing as hard as he can but getting nowhere. Then she notices that the boat has a leak and is slowly sinking.

The man is extremely busy bailing and rowing, bailing and rowing. She yells: "Hey, if you don't bring that boat ashore and fix that leak, you're going to sink!"

He replies, "Can't you see, I don't have time to fix the leak!"

The Breakfast Club members agreed that, like ships' captains, managers must occasionally go ashore and check for and fix problems—especially when we don't have the time to do it.

～☜～

A DIFFERENT PYGMALION

Have you heard of the phenomenon known as the Pygmalion effect? It happens when people perform according to expectations. More specifically, it refers to the relationships between the leader and the members of the group.

When you project confidence that your team can handle difficult tasks, it helps them to stretch themselves and live up to your expectations. Conversely, giving the impression that you hope for little more than mediocrity produces mediocrity. And taking a "there's nothing I can do about it" attitude and blaming the organization for roadblocks does the same thing.

An optimistic "can do" or a confident "I know we can do it" approach helps bolster your staff's confidence and makes good things happen. It also has another benefit. When you start to lose the wind in your sails, the team is likely to return the favor and help bolster you.

Queen Victoria had the right idea. She said, "We are not interested in the possibilities of defeat."

QUESTIONS

Have you noticed how many work-related conversations start with a question? Caring for patients, and managing the many facets of any large organization, requires innumerable exchanges of information. At first blush, a direct and specific question seems to the most efficient way to obtain information from someone. We ask a question and we get what we need. Or do we?

Take the door-to-door salesman who approaches a fenced yard. A little boy and a large German Shepherd dog are on the other side. "Is your dog friendly?" asks the man.

"Very friendly, sir," politely answers the boy. The salesman opens the gate and is immediately attacked by the dog.

"You said your dog is friendly," yells the man as he hops the fence.

"This isn't my dog," replies the child.

Here's another one. W.C. Fields did a skit in which he was a clerk in a candy store. Three youngsters walk in with pennies in hand. The first asks for a blue gum ball. The gum balls are stored on the top shelf near the very high ceiling, and Mr. Fields is forced to climb a ladder to reach them. After he puts the ladder away, the second child asks for a blue gum ball. As only he could, Mr. Fields grumbles, mumbles, and curses under his breath as he climbs the ladder for the second time. From the top, he looks down at the third boy and asks, "Do you want a blue gum ball, too?"

"No," is the reply. He puts the ladder away and "sweetly" asks the last child for his order. "I'd like a red gum ball," says the child innocently.

We improve our chances of getting the information we really need by stating the purpose of the question. Instead of "How many associates work in your department?" try "I'd like to treat your staff to doughnuts tomorrow morning. Can you tell me how many people will be here?" You're likely to get different answers to each question. More importantly, you may also find out that someone else has already planned to bring doughnuts.

Try it. The next few times you need information from a co-worker, first supply the reason you're asking. We think it will improve communication. Do you?

꧁꧂

REALLY EFFECTIVE

To be really effective, praise must be specific. A "good job" doesn't have the same positive impact as "What a creative way to present the data!"

Here are a few praise "openers" to help us be specific:

- "It made a big difference when you…"
- "You impressed several co-workers with the way you…"
- "It always helps when you…"
- "We were at a loss until you…"
- "You seem to have a knack for…"
- "You should be proud of the way you…"

Close with a sincere "Thanks."

> *We are the most impressionable creatures on God's green earth, and a kind word can set us up for a whole week.*
>
> - Sydney J. Harris

RECRUITMENT AND RETENTION

Recruitment and retention is a major priority for most companies. Along those lines:

St. Peter greets a new arrival at the Pearly Gates. He says the person must spend a day in Heaven and a day in Hell and then decide where to spend eternity. She visits Hell first and is amazed to find a beautiful golf course, perfect weather, friendly people, terrific food, and even a nice-guy devil!

Her day in Heaven is spent walking on clouds, talking to angels, listening to harps, and singing.

She tells St. Peter that Hell is more to her liking and heads south. This time she finds a desolate wasteland crowded with thirsty people filled with misery and despair. She complains to the Devil about the sudden and incredible difference. The Devil looks at her and smirks "Yesterday I was recruiting you; today you're an employee."

Hit a little too close to home? The relationship between employer and employee has changed dramatically in recent years. The demand for good associates exceeds the supply. So, unlike the poor soul mentioned above, good employees are often tempted to leave their employer. Savvy managers know new associates can easily be lured away. So they "re-recruit" them for months after they have been hired; and they continue to "court" old-timers as well.

All of us are painfully aware of the financial and emotional costs of high turnover. In fact, many managers say a major cause of stress is worrying about losing key associates.

᠅

REFLECTIONS

During one of our final meetings of the year, the Breakfast Club members discussed plans for next year's articles. We also talked about our New Year's resolutions.

A member acknowledged it is important to look forward but emphasized it is equally important to look backward now and then.

She reminded us that our work-a-day world of meetings, e-mails, projects, voice mails, and deadlines keep us future focused. But we can all benefit from a look back at how much we've accomplished during the last year. She proposed that each team's first staff meeting of a new year include a pleasant look back at the previous year.

> *To look backward for a while is to refresh the eye, to restore it, and to render it the more fit for its prime function of looking forward.*
>
>   - Margaret Fairless Barber

᠅

RELATING TO PEOPLE

One of the Breakfast Club members retired a few months ago. "I'll miss the relationships," she said on her last day of work.

Her comment got the Breakfast Club members talking about work relationships. We came up with this hierarchy:

- Competitor: someone whose goals conflict with your own
- Acquaintance: you know one another's names and say hello in the hallways
- Teammate: you're committed to a common goal and freely discuss work issues
- Friend: someone you enjoy spending time with and whose opinion you respect and seek out
- Good friend: someone you'd be willing to help late into the night in order to get them out of a work-related jam. They'd do the same for you.

You may use different terms to describe relationships, and you could probably add to the list. At any rate, a good way to improve a relationship is to treat the person as if they were one step higher on the relationship ladder.

Chances are, they'll reciprocate.

> *If you treat people right they will treat you right — ninety percent of the time.*
>
> - Franklin D. Roosevelt

⌒⌒

RELATIONSHIPS

Perhaps you've heard of Tom Peters. He co-wrote a bestseller, *In Search of Excellence* (1982), which highlighted best practices among successful corporations. He then went on the lecture circuit promoting the book's ideas to business executives. At any rate, he's credited with saying, "All business decisions hinge ultimately on conversations and relationships."

The Breakfast Club members think the micro equivalent is, "A company's effectiveness is greatly influenced by the quality of conversations and relationships its managers have with associates and with one another."

What do you think? Are our relationships important? If so, how do you go about strengthening your relationships with other managers?

P.S.: A member of the Breakfast Club research staff just handed us another befitting quote: "As organizations abandon their hierarchical structures, managers will have to rely less on the authority inherent in their title and more on their relationships with players in their informal networks. Understanding relationships will be the key to managerial success." This is from an article in the *Harvard Business Review* by David Krackhardt and Jeffrey Hanson.

⌒⌒

RELATIONSHIPS REDUX

Have you noticed the Breakfast Club articles have been aimed at helping us build effective, efficient, and fun work teams? One member compares our managers to a circular steel chain with many links. Each link consists of a work team managed by one of us. Our job is to keep our link in tiptop shape. Executive management provides overall plans, resources, and encouragement.

A strong link needs well-trained, experienced team members. Uh-oh! We imagine some of you are thinking that high associate turnover makes that impossible. Some readers may even wonder "Why get to know and train people when they will probably leave soon anyway?"

A catch twenty-two? Maybe new associates leave because they don't feel very welcome. Perhaps they suspect they won't be well trained.

We agree it's hard for managers to find the time and energy to give associates, especially new ones, the attention they want and deserve. But relationships are vitally important in all parts of life. Is it possible workers often leave employers or departments not because of the work, but because of unrewarding relationships? After all, we do spend a large percent of our waking hours on the job interacting with coworkers.

Consider this paradoxical statement: "A great place to work except for the people."

❧

Reward and Recognition

"Grandma did it again," announced a member as she joined our meeting.

"No doubt another gift situation," remarked another member.

"Yes, bless her heart."

It seems our colleague's daughter celebrated her thirteenth birthday, and grandma paid a visit with gifts in hand. She brought a very nice iPod— so far, so good. Grandma proudly said it came preloaded with every Beatle song ever recorded.

After Grandma left, the birthday girl asked, "Mom, who are the Beatles?"

The way we reward and recognize associates can become stale, too.

❧

Rockin' Runway

"My nephew is a young naval officer who was recently assigned to an aircraft carrier," announced a member as he joined our meeting a few weeks ago. "In this letter he quotes a veteran officer. Listen to this:

> 'So you want to understand an aircraft carrier? Well, just imagine that it's a busy day, and you shrink San Francisco Airport to only one short runway and one ramp and gate. Make planes take off and land at the same time, at half the present time interval, rock the runway from side to side, and require that everyone who leaves in the morning returns that same day. Then turn off the radar to avoid detection, impose strict controls on radios, fuel the aircraft in place with their engines running, put an enemy in the air, and scatter live bombs and rockets around. Now wet the whole thing down with salt water and oil, and man it with twenty-year-olds, half of whom have never seen an airplane close up. Oh, and by the way, try not to

kill anyone.'"

That incredible description prompted the Breakfast Club staff to do some research. We found out Lloyds of London has called the flight deck of an aircraft carrier the most dangerous four acres in the world. Yet things go incredibly "right" virtually all of the time. Researchers from the University of California, Berkeley recently tried to find out why. Any ideas about what they discovered?

∽≈∾

ROLES – FROM A TO …

A few more of the many roles managers play:

- advocate
- detective
- diplomat
- equipment technician
- financial advisor
- friend
- marriage counselor
- mediator
- mentor
- mother
- peacemaker
- plumber
- politician
- psychologist
- referee
- repair person
- ring master
- security guard
- sounding board

This list is pretty good evidence that being a manager is a tough job that requires a lot of flexibility. Looks like a sense of humor helps too.

∽≈∾

ROLES

The Breakfast Club members treated themselves to the afternoon off last

Wednesday. We had lunch then saw the movie *The Nutty Professor*, in which Eddie Murphy plays numerous roles.

We agreed that playing different roles is nothing new to managers. We figure a manager usually plays a wide variety of demanding roles during the average week at work. Here are a few we came up with:

- Coach
- Subject Matter Expert (had to be coined by a consultant)
- Role Model
- Leader
- Organizer
- Delegator
- Career Counselor
- Listener

We've intentionally listed just a few. We'd like you to send us more ideas. We'd also like to receive anecdotes about the kind of roles you've played in your career as a manager. We're thinking there might even be a prize for the most entertaining story.

P.S.: Just kidding about taking the afternoon off.

❦

SANTA IS A LEADER

This week's Breakfast Club team meeting included an icebreaker about our holiday plans. We filled one another in on who was traveling and who was staying in town. We also talked about family traditions.

One member told us about the booklet "The Leadership Secrets of Santa Claus." One chapter was a letter from the elves to Santa Claus. They told Santa how much they looked forward to his regular visits to the toyshop. They liked it when he chatted with each one to see how things were going. And how he really listened.

They thought it was great that he asked about problems, challenges, and obstacles. They especially liked it when he asked what he could do to help, and then did those things that were reasonable and appropriate. He even chipped in and gave them a helping hand if necessary.

With those things in mind, none of the Breakfast Club members was surprised that Santa never fails to make his December twenty-fifth deadline.

❦

"I caught my VP talking to himself again," cheerfully announced a member as he joined our group.

Of course, other members gleefully joined in with barbs about executives.

"Perhaps he does what I do," contributed another member. "When I want something to 'stick,' I say it out loud. It helps me remember facts, like a meeting location, that I might otherwise quickly forget."

᎙

Say "Thank You"

Now and then managers have the privilege of sharing good news with associates. It may be a pay raise or bonus or gift cards. This gives the manager the chance to take a few minutes to thank and acknowledge personal and team effort. Here are a few tips:

1. Be sincere. If you find it difficult to say something positive to an associate, don't try it.

2. Mention specific successes. Here are a few praise "openers":
   - "It made a big difference when you…"
   - "You impressed several co-workers with the way you…"
   - "It always helps when you…"
   - "We were at a loss until you…"
   - "You seem to have a knack for…"
   - "You should be proud of the way you…"

3. It may help to identify successes if you think in terms of:
   - Timeliness
   - Accuracy
   - Dependability
   - "Can do" attitude
   - Creativity
   - Initiative

4. Consider mentioning:
   - How your team's work contributes to the overall success of the organization.
   - How important our industry is to our family, friends, co-work-

ers, and neighbors.

Thanks for reading this book.

Brains, like hearts, go where they are appreciated.
- Robert McNamara

∽⊶∾

SCARLETT O'HARA SYNDROME

"Darn, another weekend over, and I didn't trim my hedges," announced a member as he joined our group.

He went on to say "I've spent more energy fretting over the chore than it would have taken to actually do it."

We agreed that postponing tasks, at home or at work, is stressful and unproductive. We also agreed it's wise to start the day with the least pleasant task and "Git-R-Done." It makes the rest of the day more enjoyable.

Nothing is so fatiguing as the eternal hanging on of an uncompleted task.
- William James

∽⊶∾

SKUNKWORKS

One of our members knows the ropes within our organization. If one of us needs the quick help of another department, we turn to her. She makes a strategically placed phone call or two and suddenly the issue is resolved.

Her secret? In addition to a winning personality, she tries to eat lunch in the cafeteria as often as she can. Her lunch breaks enable her to network, make friends, and pick up on the latest scuttlebutt. She puts those relationships and "insider knowledge" to good use.

Her approach reminds us of something Theodore Levitt, former editor of the Harvard Business Review, said in his book *Thinking about Management.* He wrote "In most organizations, the really new things get accomplished mostly by subterfuge and cunning. They get started in the organizational underground...."

We think things in general get done best through strong, often informal, relationships.

∽⊶∾

Shackelton's Adventure

In a previous article we mentioned Sir Ernest Shackelton. To refresh your memory, he led a twenty-seven man crew on an ill-fated expedition to Antarctica in 1914. Several movies about the expedition have been featured on television and in theaters.

On Sunday, the Breakfast Club staff went to a museum to see *Shackelton's Antarctic Adventure: The greatest survival story of all time.*

The movie and exhibit were educational, entertaining, inspirational, and motivational.

Shackelton's leadership skills have recently begun to attract much attention and study because, under the most trying of circumstances, he kept order and high morale. One way he did that was through total commitment to his men before any thought of personal gain.

No doubt, many of you have seen one of the movies. Please share with us some of the leadership skills you observed.

∽⧫∾

Share Your Ideas

One of our articles stressed how important it is for associates and managers to share ideas with one another. Several members suggested their boss is not really interested in hearing from them.

The Breakfast Club members discussed the issue. First, in fairness to managers, it is impractical to expect every idea from every associate to be worthwhile. On the other hand, most ideas do deserve a fair hearing. That's probably where we, as managers, frequently fail. When we discuss problems and solutions with associates, we increase the risk of losing control. After all, it is much easier, less time-consuming, and less stressful to simply take charge and tell others what to do.

Managers can easily slip into an authoritarian role and delude themselves into thinking they have all the answers. Chances are, the people actually doing the work have many good ideas that, unfortunately, go unmentioned because it is easier, less time-consuming, and less stressful to simply remain silent.

One way out of this vicious cycle is for the boss to regularly ask the staff to help solve problems. Involvement generates commitment that generates teamwork that generates success.

∽⧫∾

Sharpen Your Pencil

"I found another 'Details, Details' story," proudly announced our intern as he joined last week's Breakfast Club meeting.

"Entertain us," eagerly replied another member. Here's the story:

A well-meaning organization decided to communicate a clear anti-drug message to young people. It gave away thousands and thousands of pencils imprinted with the slogan "Too Cool to Do Drugs." Good idea, right? Of course, there is more to the story.

A ten-year-old noticed something the adults had failed to uncover in developing their plan. When a pencil was sharpened a few times, the message turned into "Cool to Do Drugs." When it was sharpened a few more times, the slogan became the command "Do Drugs."

The student who discovered the gaffe said this about the adults who ran the project: "I guess they didn't sharpen their pencils."

The Breakfast Club staff agreed that, because good ideas can come from everywhere (even ten-year-olds), it's a good practice to include customers in each stage of a project.

We also decided to ask ourselves several times during our projects: "Did we sharpen the pencils?"

⤖

Shine A Light

"I feel like a klutz," announced a member as he joined last week's meeting. After we concurred with his self-appraisal, we got the details. He struggled while converting clocks and electronic gadgets to daylight-saving time and blamed himself, a common reaction.

A member shared this quote with us, "It's a conspiracy of silence," says Don Norman, a leader in the burgeoning movement to make things easier to use and the author of *The Design of Everyday Things*. He argues that we're victims of our own shame: "When things don't work right, we all think it's our own fault, and nobody admits having trouble, so nothing changes."

We transferred that concept to organizational behavior. We wondered what processes great organizations use to encourage customers and associates to shine a light on things that don't work well.

⤖

Show Me!

In a previous article we asked our members to suggest the most common reason people leave their jobs. The answer: because they don't feel appreciated.

The Breakfast Club members got to wondering. If everyone (at all levels of every organization) wants to be appreciated by bosses and co-workers and subordinates and colleagues, why are we, apparently, so stingy with appreciation?

That led to another question: What is appreciation?

We agreed that, at its basic level, appreciation says "I respect you." At its highest level, appreciation says "I care about you."

༄

SHOW SOME APPRECIATION!

"My poor daughter got a taste of the real working world," announced a member as he joined our meeting.

"She's been in her first real job for about six months. She told me she put in many extra evening and weekend hours on a project and was very proud of the results."

Our colleague continued, "It turns out that even three weeks after she turned it in, no one mentioned the report or thanked her for the extra effort. She's so disappointed she wonders if she's working for the wrong employer."

We agreed failing to acknowledge good work easily destroys morale for a person or an entire team.

> *The great humiliation in life is to work hard on something from which you expect great appreciation, and then fail to get it.*
> - Edgar Watson Howe

༄

SHOWING UP

Management advice from Woody Allen?

One of the Breakfast Club members brought up Woody's words: "Eighty percent of success is showing up." Naturally, the Breakfast Club members prefer to believe he was talking about management success. We concluded he is advising managers to be visible, especially during difficult or stressful periods. Sure, it may be helpful if a manager can chip in, but it is also helpful if he or she simply shows up to offer encouragement, moral support, and maybe even food (remember a previous article?).

Showing up sends a strong, silent message that the manager is in tune and cares.

༄

Silence is Golden?

There is an off chance that you've noticed that governments, organizations, corporations, and even departments sometimes do, well, dumb things. Even the participants wonder how a group of intelligent, hard-working, well-meaning people ended up doing what they did.

Silence is one of the many reasons offered to explain the phenomenon. For a variety of reasons, group members sometimes become very reluctant to speak up.

The Bay of Pigs fiasco is an excellent example. Theodore Sorensen remarked, "Our meetings took place in a curious atmosphere of assumed consensus."

Arthur Schlesinger, Jr. said, "In the months after the Bay of Pigs, I bitterly reproached myself for having kept so silent during those critical discussions in the Cabinet Room, though my feelings of guilt were tempered by the knowledge that a course of objection would have accomplished little save to gain me a name as a nuisance."

Group members have an obligation to speak up. Equally important, group leaders have an obligation to encourage open and honest discussion.

～～～

Sit On It

We invited a manager to our last Breakfast Club meeting. When we asked her to join us for lunch, she graciously declined and added, "I plan to sit on the footlocker at lunch today." Of course, we asked for an explanation. Here it is:

> Major General Melvin Zais, former Commander of the 101st Airborne Division, once said in a speech to future officers, "If you'll get out of your warm house and go down to the barracks...and just sit on the footlocker...you don't have to tell 'em they're doing a great job. Just sit on the footlocker and talk to one or two soldiers and leave. They'll know that you know that they're working hard to make you look good."

～～～

SMART Buy

"I think garage sales should be outlawed," announced a member as she joined our meeting.

"Your husband, the reader, again?" responded another member. "As I recall, he likes to buy books at garage sales."

"Buying them and storing them are only part of the problem. He likes to tell me all about what he has read and learned.

"On Saturday, he paid fifty cents for a management book. He told me all about goal setting and asked me if I knew what the acronym SMART stood for relative to goal setting."

See another article for a translation.

❧

SMART Moves

In a previous article we suggested that managers "sit on the footlocker." A member asked: "What if the manager senses that her staff are not comfortable with her hanging around?"

We researched the topic and liked what we read in *Smart Moves for People in Charge: 130 Checklists to Help You be a Better Leader* by Samuel D. Deep and Lyle Sussman.

To improve the comfort level between manager and staff and to keep communication open, they suggest that managers:

- Don't "kill" the bearer of bad news.
- Remain cool when you do get bad news.
- Thank people for bad news. You can't solve a problem you don't know about.
- Manage by "wandering around."
- Don't get annoyed when staff over-informs you.
- Don't get annoyed when staff asks questions.
- Allow people to see you privately.

We'd add:
- Engage in small talk that allows people to learn about you as a person, and you about them.
- When staff brings you problems, ask them for potential solutions.

❧

SMART Revisited

We had asked for the meaning of the acronym SMART as related to goals. Our consensus:

- **S**pecific
- **M**easurable
- **A**ttainable (or Action Oriented)
- **R**ealistic (or Relevant)
- **T**ime Sensitive

⌘

SOLVE THIS

A member told us about a brainteaser that only one of two-hundred job applicants was able to solve. Here it is:

You are driving your car on a dark and stormy night when you notice three people waiting for a bus:

- An old lady who looks as if she is about to die.
- A friend who once saved your life.
- Perfect partner you have been dreaming about.

You have a small sports car and it can carry only one passenger. What do you do?

The answer appears later in this book.

⌘

CLOSE YOUR EYES AND CONCENTRATE

Although the Breakfast Club members have never actually observed it, we understand that in some organizations participants sometimes "rest their eyes" during meetings.

We recently read that the information processing speed of the brain increases between five and twenty percent when a person is standing rather than sitting. (Neuroscience folks: do you agree?)

Perhaps standing during important phone calls or short, critical meetings may improve performance. Give it a try and let us know.

P.S.: Thomas Jefferson, Ernest Hemingway, and Winston Churchill were advocates of standing while working.

⌘

TEACH ME

Recently the Breakfast Club staff was talking about the stress associated with training new associates. The pressure to "get the work done" often limits our training time. One way to reduce the learning curve, and your stress level, is to consider the learning style of the associate in training.

Typically we "teach" others in the way that we like to be taught. Our challenge is to match our teaching method to the associate's learning style. For those of us who are auditory learners, a simple explanation of a procedure is all we need. Auditory learners easily process information by listening to instructions, audio tapes, and presentations.

Visual learners, however, may not "get" your explanation. Providing a chart, poster, map, diagram, or graph with your explanation will save time and frustration. Isn't it interesting that, although most of us prefer visual learning, we rarely include visual cues in our daily interaction?

The final group prefers action! These learners appreciate any kind of hands-on demonstration. They need movement and an opportunity to handle instruments or equipment. For maximum results, remember to SHOW and TELL.

So the next time you're frustrated by an associate who doesn't seem to be "learning the ropes," try switching your teaching method. Let us know if it helps! We bet it will.

Business should be fun. Without fun, people are left wearing emotional raincoats most of their working lives. Building fun into business is vital; it brings life into our daily being. Fun is a powerful motive for most of our activities and should be a direct part of our livelihood. We should not relegate it to something we buy after work with money we earn.

- Michael Phillips

Work is much more fun than fun.

- Noel Coward

TAKE A LOOK AROUND YOU

Prior to the start of one of our meetings, a member read Lance Armstrong's comment about his Tour de France victories:

You don't really see the mountains as you ride through them. There is no time to dwell on the view, on the majestic cliffs and precipices and shelves that rise on either side of you, looming rock with glaciers and peaks, falling away into green pastures.

All you really notice is the road in front of you, and riders in back of you, because no lead is safe in the mountains.

We agreed it is often easy to wear "blinders" at work. Busy schedules, numerous tasks, and a sense of urgency make us oblivious to the pleasant side of work. Like tasks accomplished, dedicated co-workers, opportunities to use our talents, and a wide variety of interesting personalities.

How do you remind yourself to step back and appreciate the pleasant side of work?

> *"What I fear most about stress is not that it kills, but that it prevents one from savoring life."*
> - Jean-Louis Seven-Schreiber

❧

TAKE TWO

The Breakfast Club members discussed the reading we did on vacation this summer. Needless to say, back issues of *The Harvard Business Review* and *The Economist* were popular. One member re-read Daniel Defoe's *Robinson Crusoe*.

"Oh, Robinson Crusoe didn't take two," remarked the group's literary expert. Our quizzical looks prompted this reply: "He didn't take two to think it through. He cut down a large tree and carved a huge canoe that was too big for him to somehow get to the water."

Our member suggested, when making plans, to always "Take two to think it through." The "two" refers to time. A small decision may require two minutes—larger ones two hours, two days, or even two weeks. Thinking through the process is always time well spent.

In Robinson Crusoe's words about his failure: "This griev'd me heartily, and now I saw, tho' too late, the Folly of beginning a Work before we count the Cost; and before we judge rightly of our own Strength to go through with it."

❧

TAKING NOTICE

"Gosh, what a week I'm having. Seems like nothing is working for me," announced a member as he joined last week's Breakfast Club meeting.

"Have you taken an inventory of non-events?" queried the team's token optimist.

Our perplexed expressions prompted a short lecture. Here's a summary:

In our daily lives, we typically notice only exceptional events. We surely notice when our car doesn't start or when an associate calls in sick or when the computer system goes haywire. But "non-events" such as when the car starts, or the computer works, or we're at full staffing easily escape our attention.

Our optimist suggests keeping things in perspective by occasionally taking notice of the majority of times things do go our way.

⌒⌒

Skill or Talent

In an earlier article, we mentioned that developing an associate is one of a manager's major responsibilities. One way to help an associate grow at work is to encourage them to use their talents. Whereas a skill is something we acquire, a talent is something we're born with.

Using talents is uniquely pleasant. We see this joyfully expressed by hunting dogs that love to hunt and race horses that live to run. We see it in people who have a knack for keeping things organized and those who are good listeners or great teachers. Talents cry out to be used.

As managers, we make everyone's life better if we have the talented teacher teaching and the talented organizer organizing. The reverse may be to have the proverbial round peg in a square hole.

The best way to find out about an associate's talents and hopes is simply to get to know the person. You'll learn a great deal from pleasant, unhurried conversations.

The next step is to align talents with tasks. No doubt it will take time, effort, and creativity. It may even require the associate to transfer to another department. But, in the long run, the organization, the associate, and you will benefit.

⌒⌒

Targets

"Help," announced a Breakfast Club member as she joined our meeting. "I'm struggling with setting performance targets for my staff. What techniques do you use?"

"I take last year's results and bump it up a bit," replied a member.

"I increase last year's budget," suggested another member.

"I've tried all kinds of approaches, but the one I experimented with last year seemed to work best," volunteered one of our most experienced staff members. "I used techniques suggested by Dr. Gary Latham of the Rotman School of Management. He and his colleagues have done research on goal setting for thirty-five years." A lengthy question and answer session followed. Here is what we learned:

For complex or novel tasks, urging people to do their best leads to much higher performance than setting specific high outcome goals.

If skills and knowledge are lacking, set process goals, not outcome goals. So, instead of saying "Increase outcome by five percent" say "Give me five or six ways in which you are going to improve processes which will improve outcomes."

If a worker knows how to do something but lacks motivation, outcome goals help.

Set intermediate goals. Instead of a goal of writing a book in a year, a goal of a chapter a month will prevent a last minute rush to get things done.

Permitted to set their own goals, workers often set and attain goals that are higher than those the boss would have assigned unilaterally.

If you put scores up for everyone to see at a golf club or bowling alley, performance improves.

Our team's wisenheimer closed the meeting by asking, "How can you cheat in bowling?"

P.S.: When was the last time you heard the word wisenheimer?

✂⌇⌇∾

TECHNOLOGY RUN AMOK

"Doggone software," muttered a Breakfast Club member as he joined our weekly meeting. "I think our email system suddenly and without warning sent out a previous article to all managers."

"Don't be shocked," comforted the techie in the group. "As software becomes more and more complex, it becomes harder and harder for programmers to make 'improvements' without unintended results."

She's right, of course. But the same holds true for processes within large organizations. Policies and procedures also tend to become more and more complex. They quickly reach the point where no single person can predict the consequences of revising just a small part of the process. Of course, that doesn't stop organizations from "improving" processes using the tried and true "Do it fast, do it wrong, do it again" approach.

We agreed that taking the time to fully understand the current process is the best way to predict the real impact of improvements - especially on the customers.

We also think we came up with the organizational equivalent of the software industry's "Old bug out, new bug in" maxim. It's "Old problem fixed, new problem created."

⌒⌒⌒

TETANUS

"I just read another example of how important little things can be," declared a Breakfast Club member as he joined the staff meeting. Here's the story:

Health officials at a major university tested two mailings designed to encourage its seniors to get tetanus shots at the student health center. One gave straightforward information about tetanus. The other played on the students' emotions and detailed the unpleasant aspects of the disease. It even included somewhat gory photographs.

Follow-up interviews confirmed that students who received the mailing with the photographs remembered much more about the disease than the other group. However, only three percent of both groups actually visited the student health center.

The dismal results prompted a third test mailing. This time a map of the campus was included. It clearly highlighted the location of the health center and its hours of operation. Mind you, this mailing went to seniors who were undoubtedly familiar with the campus and the health center.

The results? About twenty-eight percent of the students visited the center and were inoculated!

Further study revealed that the map and hours of operations helped the students visualize how they could fit a visit into their busy schedules. Apparently, they compared their activities on the campus with the map and decided when they could stop in.

The Breakfast Club members concluded that the story contained several lessons. First, it pays to test solutions on a small scale. Second, some solutions are actually counterintuitive (seniors needing a map?). Third, really understanding your customers enables even small improvements, such as a map, to contribute mightily to success.

⌒⌒⌒

THAT'S WHY!

In response to an article about asking why, a member contributed this:

I like the story about the family who was preparing their Thanksgiving turkey. As the mother prepared the turkey breast for roasting, she cut two inches off each end. When her curious son asked why she did that, she replied because that was the way her mother always did it. The son then turned to his grandmother and asked her why she did that. The grandmother, of course replied, that was how her mother prepared the turkey. When they finally asked the great grandmother why she prepared the turkey this way, she responded, "Because it was too big to fit in our pan."

P.S.: In another article we asked if anyone knew what three-card monte is. Since no one admitted that they knew, we looked it up. It's a gambling game in which the dealer shows a player three cards, then turns them face down and moves them around, and the player must guess the position of a particular card. It is common for the dealer to cheat.

∽⧉⧉∾

The Agony of Defeat

"My wife was in a blue funk this weekend because her alma mater's football team lost its second close game in a row," announced a member as he joined our group.

Many in the room empathized with his wife (and some with him). It seems real sports fans often take losses to heart. In fact, we discussed that the "agony" of defeat is more powerful than the "thrill" of victory.

We agreed the same is true in the workplace. Errors, small and large, capture our attention but the many things that go well are often taken for granted.

We also agreed it is a manager's responsibility to acknowledge those who keep the ship afloat, day in and day out.

∽⧉⧉∾

The Control Theory

Before our last meeting began, the Breakfast Club members entertained one another with stories about our first "real job." We agreed that it was a bit challenging to establish a comfortable and effective relationship with our boss.

A member pulled out her copy of *The Control Theory Manager* by William Glasser, M.D. She said, "Glasser suggests it is the manager's responsibility, over time and as natural opportunities arise, to share things with the people they manage. Such sharing helps create a warm and friendly workplace."

Glasser suggests, as managers, we should share:

- Who we are. ("The better we know someone and the more we like what we know, the more we want to do, even enjoy doing, for that person.")
- What we stand for. (Example: "I believe no one should put another person down.")
- What we will ask the workers to do. (Example: "Be on time and ready to go to work at starting time." Of course, the manager must abide by this as well.)
- What we will not ask them to do. (Example: "I do not expect you to remain silent if you have serious concerns about the direction you think I am taking us.")
- What we will do for them. (Example: "I will do what I can to make sure you have the resources to do your job.")
- What we will not do for them. (Example: "I will not do your work for you or solve problems I think you can solve yourself.")

⌒⌒⌒

WHAT'S YOUR "L" FACTOR?

"I'm not sure why, but my father-in-law gave me the book *The Likeability Factor* by Tim Sanders," announced a member as he joined our meeting.

Other members quickly lowered their heads and took a sudden interest in their shoes: you get the picture.

According to the book:

> *When people encounter you, they subconsciously ask themselves four questions that determine your likeability or "L-factor." First, they seek friendliness. Then, they ask themselves if you are relevant to them. Next, they ponder whether you have empathy for them. Finally, they ask themselves if you are "real" — that is, authentic and honest. If the answers to those four questions are affirmative, you receive a high likeability factor.*

Research at Columbia University shows that likeability is an important factor in hiring, promotion, and pay decisions.

⌒⌒⌒

THE "L" FACTOR – EMPATHY

This continues our discussion of the book *The Likeability Factor* by Tim Sanders.

The book states:

> *When people encounter you, they subconsciously ask them-*
> *selves four questions that determine your likeability or "L-fac-*
> *tor." First, they seek friendliness. Then, they ask themselves if*
> *you are relevant to them. Next, they ponder whether you have*
> *empathy for them. Finally, they ask themselves if you are "real"*
> *- that is, authentic and honest. If the answers to those four ques-*
> *tions are affirmative, you receive a high likeability factor.*

Empathy is the ability to see things from another person's point of view. When you are able to connect with people's feelings and they sense that, it is the equivalent of a psychological hug.

And who doesn't need a hug now and then?

◡◠◡

The "L" Factor – Friendliness

In a previous article we mentioned *The Likeability Factor* and how we appreciate and value friendliness in others—perhaps especially at work.

Friendliness is communicated in verbal and body language. We tend to like others who are open and welcoming. And that is communicated with eye contact, a smile, cheerfulness, and positive words and body language.

People respond to friendliness. Research shows that friendly people enjoy better customer service from doctors, lawyers, waiters, and just about everyone.

◡◠◡

The "L" Factor – Realness

This continues our discussion of the book *The Likeability Factor* by Tim Sanders.

The book states:

> *When people encounter you, they subconsciously ask them-*
> *selves four questions that determine your likeability or "L-fac-*
> *tor." First, they seek friendliness. Then, they ask themselves if*
> *you are relevant to them. Next, they ponder whether you have*
> *empathy for them. Finally, they ask themselves if you are "real"*
> *- that is, authentic and honest. If the answers to those four ques-*
> *tions are affirmative, you receive a high likeability factor.*

"Realness" or genuineness is consistency between your beliefs and actions. Live by your values, and your perceived realness will elevate. But if people decide you're phony, they will discount your friendliness, relevance and empathy—and probably dislike you.

"Basically, likeability comes down to creating positive emotional experiences in others," Sanders concludes. "When you make others feel good, they tend to gravitate to you."

⚬⚬⚬

THE "L" FACTOR - RELEVANCE

This continues our discussion of the book *The Likeability Factor* by Tim Sanders.

The book states:

> *When people encounter you, they subconsciously ask themselves four questions that determine your likeability or "L-factor." First, they seek friendliness. Then, they ask themselves if you are relevant to them. Next, they ponder whether you have empathy for them. Finally, they ask themselves if you are "real" – that is, authentic and honest. If the answers to those four questions are affirmative, you receive a high likeability factor.*

Relevance is how well we are connected to others' interests, wants, and needs. Of course, sharing interests helps, but so does showing a genuine curiosity about their activities inside and outside of work. Doing so helps us be aware of others' emotional needs and helps us respond to them.

⚬⚬⚬

THE LATE SEMINARIAN

"Sorry I'm late," announced a Breakfast Club member as he joined us at the last meeting. "Seems I'm always in a rush!"

"Reminds me of research I just read about," interjected the amateur psychologist in the group. Here's a summary:

Seminarians were asked to prepare a homily and then instructed to walk across campus to deliver it to an already assembled audience. Some were asked to pick any topic. Others were asked to speak about the parable of the Good Samaritan. Unbeknownst to the students, an accomplice lay on the sidewalk between the two buildings pretending to be unconscious.

In addition, some seminarians were told something like, "Oh, you're late. Better get moving." Others were told, "You're early but you might as well head over now."

Guess what controlled whether or not the students helped the "unconscious" person?

The study concluded that the only thing that really mattered was whether the student was or wasn't in a rush. Of the group who knew they had a few minutes to spare, sixty-three percent stopped. Of those in a hurry, only ten percent stopped to help.

The Breakfast Club members agreed that hurrying affects us in more ways than we may realize.

> *No man who is in a hurry is quite civilized.*
> \- Will and Ariel Durant

❧

THE PERFECT JOB

"Listen to this New Year's resolution," announced a member as she joined our meeting. "My twenty-two-year-old daughter has resolved to find the perfect job next year."

After the giggles, groans, and pained expressions subsided, we discussed the nature of work. We concluded that, despite the young lady's expectation, all jobs have parts we don't like. The "perfect" job is one we like most of the time.

> *If the profession you have chosen has some unexpected inconveniences, console yourself that no profession is without them.*
> \- Samuel Johnson

❧

THE POWER OF THREE

During our last Breakfast Club meeting, we discussed the optimum length of our articles. We decided to mention no more than three principles related to each topic. We concluded that the message gets lost if too much is covered.

"Three is the obvious choice," pronounced a member. "Three is nature's and man's basic building block," he added confidently. "In fact, the human mind has been programmed to think in terms of three."

"Examples?" requested another member.

He rattled off an extensive list. Here are a few:

- three states of matter
- three branches of government
- triumvirate
- three musketeers
- three little pigs
- triathlon
- Larry, Darryl, and Darryl
- three dog night
- three sheets to the wind
- three stooges
- tricycle
- triple threat
- shake, rattle, and roll
- triple play
- eat, drink, and be merry

We left the meeting in silent admiration of the powerful insights of our colleague.

⌘

THE RIGHT FORMULA

"*CSI* fans, we have a new TV show to enjoy," announced a member as he entered our meeting room. "I'm looking forward to watching *Numbers*—the show about solving crimes using mathematical formulas."

"Heck, math has long been used as a forensic tool for managers," replied another member.

She delighted in our quizzical expressions and quickly went on to educate us.

Everyone knows that work includes both positive and negative interactions with bosses and coworkers. A recent study found that workgroups in which positive interactions are at least three times more common than negative ones are significantly more productive than teams with a lower ratio.

No surprises there, you say. However, the study suggests there is an upper limit as well. Things can actually worsen if the ratio goes higher than thirteen to one. In other words, bosses who use a kind of "Pollyanna" approach that ignores weakness can do more harm than good.

⌘

THE RIGHT REACTION

Several members responded to our last two articles about compliments by suggesting we write something about responding to compliments and praise. This is from Frank Doerger's book *Welcome to the Real Working World*:

> *The proper reaction to praise can leave everyone feeling good. However, if you're not sure how to react to praise, kind words from the boss could backfire into an awkward moment. You may even give the impression you're rejecting the compliment. Some tips on how to gracefully accept praise:*
>
> - *Don't remain mute or downplay your accomplishment with a meek "it was nothing."*
> - *A confident "thank you" acknowledges that you're proud of your efforts. You may want to add something like "That's nice of you to say," or "That's good to hear," or "I'm glad I was able to help."*
> - *If others helped you or deserve some of the credit, a comment like "Fred and Juanita contributed a lot," shows you're a team player.*
> - *Tell those who helped you earn the praise that the boss was pleased. Let them know you appreciate their help.*

People ask you for criticism, but they only want praise.
- Somerset Maugham

⚭

THANKSGIVING

Readers,

The Breakfast Club staff wishes you a Happy Thanksgiving and thanks you for reading and responding to our articles.

We hope you find these words appropriate for this time of year:

> *What a wonderful life I've had! I only wish I'd realized it sooner.*
>
> - Sidonie Gabrielle Colette

⚭

PYGMALION EFFECT

A few issues ago we spoke of the Pygmalion effect—when people perform according to expectations.

A manager's expectations for his or her staff are greatly influenced by the manager's underlying assumptions about human nature. That's where Douglas McGregor's famous "Theory X" and "Theory Y" come in.

"Theory X" managers assume people are fundamentally lazy and irresponsible and would probably rather be doing almost anything other than working. Therefore, the manager designs the work environment around that assumption. That means lots of instruction, oversight, exhortations, and even punishment. It probably also includes micro-managing and fault-finding.

"Theory Y" managers assume people are fundamentally hard working and responsible. They recognize that work can be rewarding and fulfilling. Therefore, the work environment is characterized chiefly by support, encouragement, and a lack of fear.

The Breakfast Club staff concluded that the "X style" is alluring because it is easy and, in the short run, effective. After all, people do respond to fear, intimidation, and threats. But they probably also work less creatively, seldom take the initiative, and look to escape to a different employer or boss.

The "Y style" takes a lot more patience and discipline. But it pays off in a pleasant, yet productive, work atmosphere. In addition, the "Y style" is more open and likely to tap into the diversity of an employee population, utilizing the strengths and talents of the entire group.

The key is to take the long view and not slip into the "X style" every time a deadline is near or the stress level gets too high. What do you think?

∽☙∾

THINK OR BLINK?

Some time ago the Breakfast Club members discussed *Blink* by Malcolm Gladwell. This bestselling book theorized that our best decision-making is done on impulse, without factual knowledge or critical analysis.

During our last meeting we discussed *Think* by Michael R. LeGault. LeGault makes a case for critical thinking.

So, what's the difference between critical and non-critical thinking? Author Vincent Ryan Ruggiero believes:

- critical thinkers acknowledge what they don't know
- non-critical thinkers pretend to know more than they do

- critical thinkers regard problems and controversial issues as exciting challenges
- non-critical thinkers regard problems and controversies as nuisances and threats to their egos
- critical thinkers base judgments on evidence rather than personal preference
- non-critical thinkers base judgments on first impressions and gut reactions

∾᷈᪥∾

ARE YOU A THINKER OR A BLINKER?

In a previous article we discussed ways to support newly appointed supervisors. We decided on these top THREE, yes THREE, ways:

- Make a formal announcement so everyone who will work with the person in his or her new role knows about the promotion. Use e-mail, newsletters, meetings, and other ways to make sure the word gets out. Make sure you tell direct reports first.
- Introduce them to people they need to know. This includes people outside the organization.
- Help them understand who's who in the organization and how to get information, resources, and assistance when they need it.

We agreed that a person's first supervisory position could be stressful. Any help they get is sure to be appreciated.

∾᷈᪥∾

TIPS FOR SUCCESS

Ever wonder what some of the world's most successful entrepreneurs have said about management and their success? The Breakfast Club members did, and we uncovered these gems:

Bill Gates (founder of Microsoft):
What I do best is share my enthusiasm.

William Hewlett (Founder of Hewlett-Packard):
Managers have traditionally developed the skills in finance, planning, marketing, and production techniques. Too often the relationships with their people have been assigned a secondary

role. This is too important a subject not to receive first line attention.

Ray Kroc (Founder of McDonald's):
You're only as good as the people you hire.

John D. Rockefeller (Founder of Exxon):
Good management consists in showing average people how to do the work of superior people.

Sam Walton (founder of Wal-Mart):
What has carried this company so far so fast is the relationship that we, the managers, have been able to enjoy with our associates. By "associates" we mean those employees out in the stores and in the distribution centers and on the trucks who generally earn an hourly wage for all their hard work. Our relationship with the associates is a partnership in the truest sense. It's the only reason our company has been able to consistently outperform the competition—and even our own expectations.

Thomas J. Watson (Founder of IBM):
A manager is an assistant to his men.

~~~

TRAINING, TRAINING, TRAINING

In one of our articles, we mentioned that researchers from the University of California, Berkeley, studied aircraft carriers to find out why things go incredibly "right" virtually all of the time. Here are a few of their findings:

> *Standard operating procedures govern most activities and much of the navy training is devoted to making them second nature.*
>
> *When planes start landing and taking off, cooperation and communication become more important than orders passed down the chain of command and information passed back up. Events can happen too quickly for that. The crew members act as a team, each watching what others are doing and all of them communicating constantly through telephones, radios, hand signals, and written details. This constant flow of information helps catch mistakes before they've caused any damage.*

*Emergencies call for a third level of organizational struc-
ture. The crew has carefully rehearsed procedures for a fire on
the flight deck, for instance. Each member assumes a pre-as-
signed role and reacts immediately without direction.*

◦◦◦

Tuning In To The Max

"Well, my son finally accepted a new position," announced a member as she joined our meeting.

Our member's son had been encouraged by his boss to apply for a position with greater responsibility. The young man was uncertain of his abilities and kept postponing the move.

His wise mother shared the following quote with him and it did the trick:

> *"To find the optimum position of a worker is like operating a
> radio receiver. You wish to tune in a station very precisely. You
> have a meter that indicates signal strength and as you near the
> optimum point the needle begins to move across the dial. It is
> not until the needle passes the maximum and starts to fall back
> that you can be certain that it has reached the maximum."*
>
> - J. Goldston

We then discussed a likely scenario: an associate, with encouragement from his or her supervisor, moves to a position which turns out to be beyond his/her talents and skills. Might both the associate and the supervisor become unhappy and frustrated?

We wonder how often the once valuable associate ends up leaving the organization as a result of the promotion. A lose-lose situation?

◦◦◦

Under Watchful Eyes

"It seems like I'm reminded of Mike Abrashoff's books in the darndest ways," announced a Breakfast Club member as she joined our group. "My husband and I took advantage of this weekend's gorgeous weather by taking the children to the zoo. At the lowland gorilla exhibit, my six-year-old observed how all the members of the group kept a very, very close eye on every move made by the silverback."

She went on to say that it may be an odd comparison but associates, as Mike mentioned, also closely observe their manager's every move.

We agreed that the manager sets the tone in many ways. Honesty, integrity, respect, work ethic, openness, teamwork, and fun on the job are fashioned and maintained by the group's leader—whether he or she knows it or not.

> *Example is not the main thing in influencing others. It is the only thing.*
>
> - Albert Schweitzer

❧

USE IT OR LOSE IT!

"Hey, I spent quite a few hours at home last weekend using XtremeLearning, and I think I learned some good stuff about Microsoft Office," announced a member as she joined the Breakfast Club meeting.

"Better use that knowledge today," blurted the educator in the group.

"Why today?" was the response.

Our educator went on to say that research reveals that the chances of us ever applying training lessons that are not applied on the first day back at work range from low to nothing.

We agreed that managers must allow themselves and their helpers ample time to actually use what they've learned. One way is to consider practice time as an integral part of the learning cycle. So, if a helper is scheduled to attend a one-day training course, consider it a day and a half, with the half-day set aside for practice.

❧

ASK FOR THEIR HELP

"I was car shopping over the weekend," announced a member as she joined our meeting. She continued, "My current car is almost nine years old, and I'm impressed with the fit and finish of new cars."

"That reminds me of an automotive CQI story," added another member.

"It seems that executives and engineers were challenged to develop a new design. They started by asking those on the assembly line for ideas. One executive climbed into the beginnings of what was to become a car. As it made its way down the assembly line, he asked workers for their ideas on how to build a better vehicle. The workers came up with over a thousand ideas!"

We agreed those who actually do the work are an invaluable resource and should be included in decision-making discussions.

WAS IT WORTH IT?

"Teenagers!" announced a member as she joined our meeting.

"My son and I were in the family room. I was sitting in a chair reading and he was sitting on the sofa drinking pop and watching television. I saw him put the pop on the coffee table and lie down. He then realized he could no longer reach the pop. Instead of getting up, he hooked his foot around a leg of the coffee table and tugged. Needless to say, the glass tipped over and spilled soda on the carpet."

We laughed and agreed most shortcuts, at home or work, are actually "longcuts."

∽∾

SLICED?

The story goes something like this: A department decides to have a picnic at a swim club. The manager asks an associate to bring three large watermelons. The associate sees this as an opportunity to take the initiative. Not only does he buy the melons, he meticulously slices and wraps each piece in cellophane. He's proud of himself for thinking ahead and is sure everyone will appreciate his extra effort.

His manager groans when she sees him approaching the picnic with the slices. She had planned to throw the watermelons into the pool to play a kind of water polo with them!

The moral of the story is that willing workers do a better job when they know why they have been asked to do something.

Knowing "the why" helps us to make effective decisions about the project.

Every day throughout our hospitals, associates make thousands of requests of one another and of patients. We ask for supplies, data, equipment, information, and ideas. We assume the other person knows why we're asking. Often that assumption is wrong and causes confusion and re-work. So, whether we're at the sending or receiving end of a request, let's ask ourselves if everyone is clear about "the why."

No more sliced watermelons!

∽∾

"We" or "They" – What's Your Pronoun?

Former Secretary of Labor Robert Reich was asked, "What yardstick do you use to determine the health of an organization?"

His response:

> *When I walk into places of work, I administer what I call my pronoun test. I ask people to tell me about their place of work, to tell me what they do, and what it's like to work where they work. I don't listen so much to the content of what they say, although I'm certainly interested, I listen more for the pronouns they use. If they use "we" and "our," I know that it's a workplace that has cultivated a sense of connection between worker and enterprise. So that at some level, the employee feels that his or her fate is linked to the success of what the enterprise does. By contrast if I hear the third person pronouns, "they" or "they're," in describing the enterprise, I know it's a very different kind of place. There's less connective tissue. Employees may still feel that it's important to do a good job, but they don't feel a deep sense of connection with the organization. I've also noticed that there is an almost direct relationship between my pronoun test and enterprise performance. Almost invariably places where all employees pass my pronoun test, in the sense they use the personal pronouns "we," "our" and "us," are far more successful than enterprises where employees don't pass the pronoun test. They revert to "they" and "them" and "they're" in describing the enterprise. It's the quickest and easiest way I know to find out a lot of information.*

꧁꧂

What Are You Waiting For?

"I like the idea of posting our Core Values in meeting rooms," announced a member as she saw a plaque hanging in our meeting room.

She went on to say that one of her favorite quotes is:

> *There are many persons ready to do what is right because in their hearts they know it is right. But they hesitate, waiting for the other fellow to make the first move; and he, in turn, waits for you.*
>
> – Marian Anderson

We agreed that having the Core Values prominently displayed encourages all of us to speak up (or even just point to the plaque) during those rare awkward moments when the need arises.

P.S.: According to Answers.com, Marian Anderson was the first black person to sing in the White House (1936) and at New York's Metropolitan Opera House (1955). In 1939, the Daughters of the American Revolution prevented her from performing in a concert at Constitution Hall in Washington, DC. First Lady Eleanor Roosevelt resigned from the DAR in protest, and arranged instead for Anderson to perform at the Lincoln Memorial where seventy-five thousand turned out to hear her sing "America."

~~~

WHAT COMES FIRST – GOOD SERVICE OR TIP?

"How can siblings be so different?" asked a member as she joined our meeting.

"Now what?" inquired another member.

"My sons are just two years apart and couldn't more different," she continued. "The older one is an optimist and the younger one is a pessimist."

"They spent the summer working as servers in two different upscale restaurants. The older son probably earned three times as much in tips. He believed in being pleasant and attentive to everyone. The younger one admitted that he plans to be pleasant and attentive after he starts getting better tips!"

We agreed providing outstanding customer service isn't easy but it produces results.

~~~

WHAT IT REALLY MEANS

In a previous article we mentioned C. Northcote Parkinson. He is famous for his satire of bureaucratic institutions. His "laws" include:

- Work expands so as to fill the time available for its completion.
- Expenditure rises to meet income.
- The matters most debated in a deliberative body tend to be the minor ones where everybody understands the issues.
- When something goes wrong, do not try, try again. Instead, pull back, pause, and carefully work out what organizational shortcomings produced the failure. Then, correct those deficiencies. Only after that, return to the assault.

"Expenditure rises to meet income" is the law applicable to a previous Breakfast Club article.

⌒⌒⌒

WISH LIST

We dedicated our last Breakfast Club meeting to efficiency. Specifically, we brainstormed ways for managers to help associates generate ideas to make us even more effective and efficient. These are a few "openers" we came up with:

- If we could magically change something at work, what would it be?
- Might we be doing things that are not really necessary?
- Do we know why we do what we do?
- Do our processes make it too easy to make errors?
- Do we have data to back up our statements and suspicions about processes?

⌒⌒⌒

WHAT'S THIS?

"Story time," cheerfully announced a team member as she joined our weekly meeting.

"My sixteen-year-old daughter is working at a large discount store this summer. One of her duties is to restock the shelves. Of course, knowing on which shelf each of the thousands of products goes is a challenge.

"She came home yesterday more than a bit embarrassed. She spent fifteen minutes roaming up and down the cosmetics section trying to find out where to put 'Liquid Nails.'

"When she sought help, her boss burst out laughing. The Liquid Nails was a tube of glue used to adhere paneling to walls!"

We agreed it is far too easy to assume others naturally know everything we know about our work environment. We also agreed lots of patience and training is integral to success and high morale.

⌒⌒⌒

WHAT'S YOUR CALLING?

"I've got the Monday morning blues," announced a member as she joined our meeting.

After the commiserating stopped, a member asked, "Which category of worker are you?"

The blank stares prompted an explanation. Research by Dr. Amy Wrzesniewski showed that employees generally view work as:

- just a job, with the primary focus on financial rewards
- a career, with the primary focus on advancement
- a calling, with the primary focus on the work itself

We spoke with envy of those we know who have a calling and, if they could afford to, would continue to do the work they love even if they didn't get paid to do it.

Dr. Wrzesniewski summarized her work by stating "Satisfaction with life and with work may be more dependent on how an employee sees his or her work than on income or occupational prestige."

We agreed that health care offers all of us, regardless of our role, the right to be proud of our contribution. In fact, since all of us are totally dependent on one another to care for patients, with a good perspective, every job can become a calling. And with the right combination of energy, knowledge, humor, and compassion we can help one another find and maintain that calling.

～⌘～

WHEN DID THE PROCESS CHANGE?

"I got a lecture from my management engineering friend last weekend," mentioned a team member as he joined our meeting.

"Give us the story," requested another member.

"We have breakfast together most Saturdays, and I usually pick him up at his home. Keep in mind both of us tend to be punctual. I park in his driveway and within a minute he comes out of the house. Last Saturday, for no particular reason, I parked in front of his house. I waited and waited and finally went to his front door and rang the doorbell. He opened the door, saw my car in front of the house and exclaimed, "So, you changed the process without telling me!"

I told him I didn't know we had a process.

"Now you sound like my clients," was his reply.

Our team member went on to say that his friend always sat at the dining room table where he could see his driveway. When our team member pulled into the driveway, his friend could see the car and join him. But he could not see the street from his dining room.

He went on to say that organizations get things done through processes. Some are formal and documented. Others are informal and not documented. In either case, most people know only a part of the overall process.

And therein lays the danger. A seemingly simple change to a process (like parking in front of the house instead of the driveway), can have unexpected, expensive, and frustrating consequences – especially in a large organization.

The team agreed that every associate's mantra must be "Who needs to be consulted, or at least informed, before we make this change?"

⤮

Who Do You Trust?

In a well-received video, Lou Holtz reminds us that everyone, in every kind of relationship, wonders of others "Can I trust you?"

The Great Place to Work Institute's leaders believe "Trust is the essential ingredient for the primary workplace relationship between the employee and the employer." They also believe trust in the workplace is composed of credibility, respect, and fairness.

Those three words cover a lot of territory.

Sure, credibility means words must be followed by appropriate action. But it also means we, as managers, must regularly communicate the "big picture" to associates. That builds a sense of belonging and also enables them to suggest ways to contribute to the department's and the organization's success.

Respect means more than being cordial and professional. It includes giving associates the training and tools to do their jobs and collaborating with them on relevant decisions. Appreciating good work and extra effort reflects respect as well.

Of course, fairness must be built into everything we do: hiring, compensation, promotion, and recognition. But it also includes well-communicated processes for appealing disputes.

Any idea on how your associates would rate you on credibility, respect, and fairness?

P.S.: One of our fellow managers reminded us that responding to e-mail and returning phone calls within twenty-four hours is also a sign of respect.

⤮

Who is "They"?

"I'm a board member of a local charity," announced one of the Breakfast Club members as she walked into the Breakfast Club conference room. "Last night the CPA firm we hired gave their annual report, and I was fascinated by their use of pronouns. Instead of saying "your expenses" they said "our expenses.""

We then talked about how common it is for employees to use the word "they" when referring to their organization. Sales people often say something like "They decided to stop carrying that brand," or "They moved that item to aisle seven."

We agreed it is more pleasing to hear employees use "we" instead of "they" because "they" implies helplessness or even an adversarial relationship.

We also theorized that it may be a good way to measure morale. We suspect the word "we" suggests greater associate loyalty. The Breakfast Club staff decided to keep our ears open and see how our organization scores on the "we" factor. How do you think your department scores?

◦∽◦

Who Knew?

"Darn, this morning I arrived at 7:30 for a meeting that was canceled," announced a member as she joined our group.

"I've long made it a practice to miss meetings that have been canceled," contributed our wisenheimer.

"Very funny," continued our early riser. "The meeting was cancelled via e-mail yesterday afternoon, but I was in other meetings and didn't get the chance to read the e-mail."

We agreed that those who cancel meetings at the last minute, especially early morning meetings, can minimize confusion by using the organization's email system to make sure the cancellation message was read by everyone. If not, paging or phoning is necessary.

◦∽◦

Who's Counting?

The hardest arithmetic to master is that which enables us to count our blessings.

- Eric Hoffer

◦∽◦

WHO WANTS TO MEET?

"So, who's surprised," mumbled a Breakfast Club member as she glanced at a "*USA Today* Snapshot" graph.

She continued, "Harris asked about three thousand people 'What makes you feel unproductive at work?' The clear winner was unfocused meetings."

We assigned a task force to recommend five significant ways to improve meetings. They suggested:

- have an agenda and stick to it
- open the meeting by stating what you hope to achieve in the meeting
- encourage everyone to participate and discourage anyone from dominating the discussion
- close the meeting by summarizing what has been accomplished. Ask each participant to state what they are going to do and when
- distribute minutes as soon as practical

∾᠅∾

WHY?

"Be kind to me today," announced a member as she joined our meeting.

"Now what?" asked our curmudgeon.

"I babysat my two-year-old grandson all day Saturday and Sunday. If he asked 'why?' once, he asked it two hundred times. I'm exhausted."

"Bring him to work," commanded another member. "Every organization needs people to challenge the status quo by asking why."

An animated conversation followed. We agreed that asking why fosters creativity and organizational improvement. We also agreed that pat answers are often given in response to the first "why?" It's important to ask why to each successive answer in order to get to the heart of the matter. One member likened it to Russian Nesting Dolls or even three-card monte.

∾᠅∾

WHY? WHY? WHY?

"My three-year-old seems to ask 'why?' fifty times a day," announced one of the Breakfast Club staff members as we waited to begin the last staff meeting of 2001. "The first signs of a great Total Quality Manager," replied another member.

Our quizzical looks prompted an explanation. "The CQI rule of thumb is to ask 'why?' five times. In other words, to each answer ask 'why' again."

She then shared this story: a young man who worked for a tire manufacturer asked why tires were wrapped in paper before shipping. He was told, none too politely, that it prevented the whitewalls from getting scuffed and dirty. Most of us would have let it go at that, but this young man persisted.

He discovered that the manufacturer began wrapping tires about forty years ago when wide whitewalls were all the rage. But today, the vast majority of customers don't prefer whitewalls. In addition, the stripes are usually very narrow and not likely to get marred in shipping. The company stopped wrapping tires and saved twenty-two million dollars.

> *There is nothing so useless as doing efficiently that which should not be done at all.*
> - Peter F. Drucker

P.S.: This and other interesting lessons can be found in the book *Sacred Cows Make the Best Burgers* by Robert Kriegel and David Brandt.

∽∾∾

WINDOW ON THE WORLD

"The Web sure is a window on the world," announced our Internet junkie as she joined our meeting.

"Now what have you learned?" asked our self-described Luddite.

Our researcher went on to say that in 1999 The Hudson Institute performed a survey and concluded that these were the six work factors that have the highest influence on employees' commitment to their workplace:

- Fairness at Work (includes fair pay)
- Care and Concern for Employees
- Satisfaction with Day-to-Day Activities
- Trust in Fellow Associates and Supervision
- Reputation of the Organization
- Interesting Work and Job Resources

We discussed the kinds of "fairness," beyond pay, associates expect.

P.S.: What the heck is a Luddite?

∽∾∾

At this time of the year we can count on several of the Breakfast Club staff members to reminisce about their high school football careers. A new member shared this: "I was not athletic, so I signed up for the intramural team. What a rude awakening. I joined for the camaraderie and a little exercise. Everyone else seemed to be intent on winning. Needless to say, I didn't enjoy it very much."

"Yep, different aims are a great source of pain and conflict," continued another member. "We see it at home, school, work, and every level of politics. Sounds like you aimed to have fun but the others aimed to win. Too bad that wasn't clear at the onset."

We agreed that the aim of every work team in an organization must be communicated to everyone, especially newcomers. It's much too easy to assume everyone is fully aware of the work team's purpose, values, roles, and responsibilities. Without statements (and reminders) like "We're here to cooperate with one another and other departments to help improve the health of our community" some may have the outmoded notion that the team exists to look out for its own best interests.

Clear values and aims help members make decisions that are good for them, the team, and the organization.

> *When you identify with your company's purpose, when you experience ownership in a shared vision, you find yourself doing your life's work instead of just doing time.*
>
> — John Naisbitt and Patricia Aburdene

⌒⌒

You Can Keep Your Monkey

"Remember the last Breakfast Club article about subordinate-imposed time," asked a member as she joined our meeting. "Well," she continued, "I jokingly asked my VP if I could 'move a monkey from my back' to hers. To her credit, she used my attempt at humor to tactfully broach the topic in a more serious tone."

Our team member then shared with us the results of their heart-to-heart conversation. In effect, our team member will bring issues to her VP, but with three or so suggested courses of action. They would discuss the options, and the VP would share her experience and guidance, but the manager still had to leave the office with the "monkey on *her* back" and not on the VP's.

We agreed that a good leader helps subordinates grow by shaping potential options but allowing the subordinate to make the decision.

∽ᐱᕐᐱᑦ

ARE YOU SEA-WORTHY?

Imagine this: you are a thirty-six-year-old career Navy officer given command of your first ship. It is armed with every cutting-edge system available and is worth hundreds and hundreds of millions of dollars. It has a crew of three hundred ten highly skilled men and women. Naturally, you are thrilled to be entrusted with such responsibility.

Now the bad news. The ship had been experiencing exceptionally low morale and unacceptably high turnover. The ship's "readiness indicators" were not encouraging. Keep in mind, you can't hand out pay raises and have no say in the kind of benefits offered your crew. You are also handcuffed to the notoriously rigid hierarchy of the Navy.

Do you think it's possible, within two years, to quantitatively improve every aspect of your ship? Even to the point that it becomes regarded as the finest ship in the Pacific Fleet?

What two or three things would you do during your first few weeks in command?

∽ᐱᕐᐱᑦ

BETTER LATE THAN NEVER

A member sent us this insightful response to the Breakfast Club's article about compliments:

> *Maybe it's impossible to notice everything immediately. If we pay a compliment, and the person comes back with a comment that points out that we missed something (i.e., "this was the third time you've seen me wear this blouse," or "these curtains have been here two weeks") then it might be good to know how to respond when this happens.*
>
> *For example, we could be ready to say, "I'm sorry it took me two weeks to notice, and I still like the new curtains!" or, "Did it take me three times to see this blouse before I noticed and said something? I'm sorry, and I still like your blouse!"*
>
> *In other words, I don't think we should let our possible lateness in noticing stop us from reinforcing those things we've noticed, even if we might be late! Some might then be intimidated and not comment at all, and I think this would be worse than a late comment. If we can maintain a sense of humility and*

∽⚬∾

CHANGES

Marcus Aurelius Antoninus made this observation about 1,800 years ago: "The universe is change…"

Every worker can attest — the pace of change has increased considerably since he ruled Rome.

Sooner or later, all of us are affected in some way by changes imposed in the workplace. Here is an overview of the five stages of change we are likely to experience:

STAGE 1 – Also known as the "Oh no" stage
- Mind goes blank
- People cannot even imagine how that will look or feel or be like
- People may experience:
  - Shock
  - A sense of fear
  - Outrage
  - Betrayal
  - Denial

STAGE 2 – The "Now what" stage
- This is where a person's brain starts adjusting
- A list of problems that have arisen from the change may come up in people's consciousness
- At this stage some people will react with
  - This is impossible, it can't be done
  - Hmm, maybe I can do this

If Stage 2 is handled appropriately, then groups can proceed to Stage 3

STAGE 3 – The "What, where, how on earth?" stage
- This is the early problem-solving stage
- The first true "when, where, how" questions come to mind—but, perhaps, not yet any answers

STAGE 4 – The "That's how we will try to do this" stage
- Here focus shifts so that true (problem-solving) questions are asked and true (problem-solving) answers are beginning to form and snowball

STAGE 5 – The "This is how we do things" stage
- New reality becomes permanent
- The cycle starts over

ᴄᴀᴄ

DELEGATION 101

"Yikes, I think I'm treating my team members like my father treated me as a child," announced a member as he joined our meeting. He continued, "Every time I started a chore like washing the car, he would take over because he could do it better."

That turned the conversation to the art of delegating. Many of us wondered if we delegated enough.

Here is an excerpt from an article by Paul M Ingevaldson that appeared in the March 24, 2008, edition of *Computerworld*:

> *If your subordinate comes to you with an easy question, then there are two possibilities. First, the subordinate doesn't have the confidence to make the decision and wants validation from you, the boss. In this case, you must be careful not to answer the question but to tell the subordinate that he should trust his own instincts and make the call. In this way, he will have an opportunity to grow as a person and will begin to gain the confidence that he's lacking. You also will be able to monitor his decision-making ability.*
>
> *The second possibility is that the answer was indeed simple but you didn't share the necessary information, requiring the subordinate to ask the question. This may mean you retain some information in order to feel that you have not lost control, but it causes your people to be frustrated and to feel that you don't trust them. It's important for you to disclose to your subordinates all of the information that they need to do their jobs.*

We agreed to give it a try. After all, how we delegate is key to every manager's success.

P.S.: Paul M. Ingevaldson retired as CIO at Ace Hardware Corp. in 2004 after forty years in the IT business.

ᴄᴀᴄ

Devil's Advocate?

A member expanded on the difficulties of "speaking up." She suggested we want to avoid:

- Being seen as foolish
- Embarrassing other members
- Angering other members or "higher ups"
- Fear of negative consequences

But trying to minimize conflict and reach consensus without critically testing, evaluating, and analyzing ideas can easily result in hasty, even irrational, decisions.

Such "groupthink" has been extensively studied and experts suggest a variety of ways to avoid it. The one we find intriguing is to assign a member the role of "devil's advocate." That is, someone who takes a position for the sake of argument and to avoid groupthink. The role should be rotated among members at each meeting.

⌘

Did You Use It After You Asked?

A previous article suggested asking frontline workers for improvement ideas and including them in decision-making discussions. We used the example of the many ideas generated in making a new car.

Here is a member's insightful response:

> *Perhaps a follow-up would be to learn how many of those ideas were actually implemented. If an idea was not used, were the workers told why? Employees are flattered, honored, and excited when asked their opinion, but that later turns to frustration when it appears nothing was done or there was no follow-up as to why something was not feasible or practical. Sometimes just explaining why or why not makes a big difference.*

Your approach to gracefully rejecting an idea?

⌘

Do You Multi-Task? Should You?

"Phooey to multi-tasking," announced a member as she joined us.

Turns out she read about an interesting experiment. Two participants were given five minutes to complete as much as possible of the following tasks: fry an egg to perfection, count backwards in sevens, make a cup of tea, arrange the letters of the alphabet in order on the table and respond to incoming text messages and phone calls.

One participant bragged that she was a born multi-tasker. She tried to do everything at once, and got muddled while counting backwards (in her defense, she claimed to be poor at mental arithmetic). She was roundly defeated by her opponent's sequential approach.

Countless experiments have shown that it is better to do one task after another. Stephen Monsell, a professor of cognitive psychology at Exeter University, says this is because switching between tasks increases the overall time to get the tasks done by about a third.

P.S.: During our meeting, we think we observed one of our members zero-tasking!

~~~

Don't Even Try Dozing Here!

"Yikes, I'm not sure but I think I dozed off in the meeting I just left," announced a member as she joined our meeting.

"I doubt if that happened in Alfred Sloan's meetings," responded another member who proceeded to give us a bit of a history lesson.

Alfred Sloan headed General Motors from the 1920s until the 1950s and was a highly regarded executive with an effective meeting format. At the start of the meeting, he announced the meeting's purpose. Then he listened and spoke only when necessary to clarify confusing points. At the end of the meeting he summed up, thanked everyone, and left. He immediately wrote a memo to the participants summarizing the discussion. It included responsibilities and deadlines.

We agreed a fast-paced meeting with a predictable format probably kept snoozing to a minimum.

~~~

Lookin' Good - Maybe

"I have mixed emotions about the coming of warm weather," announced a member as she joined our Breakfast Club meeting.

"Why?" queried another member incredulously.

"Warm weather brings with it lots of questions about our dress code. And some associates seem to stretch the definition of business causal," was the reply.

Another member pulled out a recent copy of the *Harvard Business Review* and read aloud part of an article. It went something like this:

> *Many years ago, a Mayo Clinic associate was asked by her supervisor to clean her shoelaces! The associate was highly offended and argued that she didn't have direct patient contact, so why should it matter?*
>
> *Her boss said that she had contact with Mayo customers in ways she may not have thought of—as she ran errands on her way home from work while wearing her Mayo name tag, or passing patients and their families in the parking lot, or in the halls of the building.*
>
> *Over time the associate realized that everything she did, even down to the shoelaces she wore to work, represented her commitment to Mayo's patients and visitors.*

We agreed that times have changed. Nurses used to wear caps and many men used to wear ties to work. But we also agreed that the way we dress is especially important in health care. Clothing is something a customer can see, whereas medical expertise and technical ability aren't. Like it or not, patients often make sweeping assumptions about us based simply on the way we dress (or how clean our buildings are).

Of course, many departments are off-limits to customers. That doesn't diminish the importance of dress, however. Each of us is an ambassador for our department and our manager. Savvy associates recognize that and take their dress cues from their managers.

We also agreed that each manager must maintain the proper dress standard in his or her department. Failing to do so makes it hard on all other managers because associates may see others in "super casual dress" and assume it is now considered appropriate.

~~~

EFFECTIVE LEADERSHIP

"My daughter, who is working on her MBA, has become very interested in the wisdom and teachings of Peter Drucker," announced a member as he joined our meeting.

Peter Drucker is known as the father of modern management. A prolific writer, business consultant and lecturer, he introduced many management concepts that have been embraced by corporations around the world.

He believed there is no such thing as a stereotypical leader—they are "all over the map in terms of their personalities, attitudes, values, strengths, and weaknesses." However, he thought effective leaders followed the same eight practices. They:

- asked, "What needs to be done?"
- asked, "What is right for the enterprise?"
- developed action plans
- took responsibility for decisions
- took responsibility for communicating
- were focused on opportunities rather than problems
- ran productive meetings
- thought and said "we" rather than "I"

We were especially interested in running productive meetings.

~~∾

EFFECTIVE MEETINGS

A previous article asked members for tips on managing effective meetings. Here's what we received:

- Avoid a meeting if a memo, e-mail, or brief report is equally effective.
- Draft and distribute a preliminary agenda. Revise it based on feedback.
- If the meeting is called to make a decision, make sure the appropriate decision makers will be present.
- Start on time.
- Leave "rank" at the door.
- Follow the detailed, prioritized agenda.
- Control off-topic conversations that some participants may be involved in. Calling time-out is one approach.
- Most meetings need a person for each of these roles:
  Leader convenes the meeting
  Facilitator helps keep the meeting moving along
  Recorder takes notes
  Timekeeper reminds leader when time is almost up for a given item.

- Encourage participation from everyone.
- At the end of the meeting, reiterate the "to do" list.
- End on time and on a positive note.
- Shortly after the meeting, send email to remind everyone of his or her responsibilities.

⁓⊶⊷⁓

FRUSTRATION AT WORK

We received several responses to our request about how to deal with frustration at work:

> *Understanding the personality of the people you work with, manage or report to is less frustrating if you have some understanding of their personality type. For example: if you need to describe a problem, some people prefer a telephone call, some an email (so they can better keep track of it), while some prefer to discuss the problem face to face. A better "personal connection" usually results in less frustration, which results in a happier, more productive workplace.*

A member finds it helps to refer to "Finish Every Day" by Ralph Waldo Emerson:

> *Finish every day and be done with it.*
> *You have done what you could.*
> *Some blunders and absurdities no doubt have crept in.*
> *Forget them as soon as you can.*
> *Tomorrow is a new day.*
> *Begin it well and serenely and with too high a spirit,*
> *To be cumbered with your old nonsense.*
> *This day is all that is good and fair.*
> *It is too dear, with its hopes and invitations,*
> *To waste a moment on yesterdays.*

A member suggested maintaining realistic expectations. He believes it helps to expect that most days will include interruptions, new problems, misunderstandings, and unanticipated tasks. To expect otherwise is to invite frustration.

One member suggests putting a name to our reactions. She suggests that saying to ourselves "This is making me frustrated" helps mitigate the feeling.

Go Where The Action Is

"I get a kick out of playing fetch with Georgie, my dog," remarked a member before our meeting began. "I tell her I'm ready to play and she runs all over the house looking for her favorite ball."

"That's a characteristic of a good manager," replied another member.

After our quizzical looks subsided, he explained that good managers make a habit of roaming about the workplace. We agreed that meetings and written or computer reports are abstractions. Leaders must go where the action is and see for themselves how things are going. After all, things change. The assumptions used to make previous decisions could easily be outdated. And associates like a visible leader who has the "common touch."

> *The answers are never in the numbers. You have to get out and look.*
> - A.G. Lafley, one time CEO of Proctor and Gamble

༄༅

Help Out – It Feels Good!

"I'm looking forward to participating in this year's fund raising event at the nonprofit where I volunteer," announced a member as he joined our meeting. "I volunteered last year," he continued, "and was glad I could help. It felt very rewarding."

"Sounds like you experienced 'helper's high,'" remarked another member.

She then educated us on research related to volunteerism. She quoted Stephen Post, a professor at the Case Western Reserve University School of Medicine, as saying "There is now a convergence of research leading to the conclusion that helping others makes people happier and healthier."

༄༅

Humor Helps

"The pro football season is only a couple weeks old and my husband has already told me his favorite football story—three times," announced a member as she joined our meeting.

"Tell us the story," replied another member with a bit too much enthusiasm for a Monday morning.

Here's what we learned:

It's the 1989 Super Bowl with the Cincinnati Bengals playing the San Francisco 49ers. Cincinnati is ahead sixteen to thirteen with just 3:20 left in the game. Joe Montana, the San Francisco quarterback, recognizes that his players are much too nervous and uptight and he needs to break the tension. In the huddle he says, "There, in the stands, standing near the exit ramp, isn't that John Candy?" The players look at the sidelines and then return their attention to their quarterback, who they thought had lost his mind. Laughter erupts in the huddle, and the tension evaporates.

The 49ers scored the winning touchdown with thirty-four seconds to spare.

We agreed with Edward Abbey when he said: "When the situation is desperate, it is too late to be serious. Try playfulness."

✂

IMPORTANT OR URGENT?

Many of our articles are about getting things done. After our last meeting, several Breakfast Club team members confessed to bad habits such as:

- compulsively checking e-mail and voice mail
- trying to get the endless list of "little" tasks done before tackling "big" tasks
- being "always available" to others which makes it hard to focus on important tasks

Experts have long suggested we prioritize our work. That was never easy and e-mail, voice mail, and cell phones have made it even more difficult. They allow the urgent to displace the important.

Steven Covey describes a high-level prioritization scheme in his book *The Seven Habits of Highly Effective People*. In this scheme, tasks are categorized this way:

- Important and Urgent
- Important but Not Urgent
- Not Important but Urgent
- Not Important and Not Urgent

Dr. Covey notes that highly effective people make time for the Important but Not Urgent activities, which can reduce time spent in other activities.

One Breakfast Club member is experimenting with spending the first hour of each day on Important but Not Urgent tasks. She closes the door, does not read e-mail, and does not answer the phone. Instead, she thinks and plans and works on important things.

> *Men have become the tools of their tools.*
> - Henry David Thoreau

> *The urgent problems are seldom the important ones.*
> - Dwight D. Eisenhower

INBOX OVERLOAD

"Darn e-mail," announced a member as he joined our meeting. "I returned from vacation to find my inbox jammed with at least a million e-mails."

That prompted an e-mail one-upmanship contest. Someone claimed to receive a million e-mails a day!

We did get serious and discussed the best way to tackle the inbox after being away from the office.

Some suggested opening the most recent e-mails first because some of them may eliminate the need to open earlier messages. For instance, a message that says something like "I found the answer to the question I had posed in an earlier e-mail." If you read the oldest e-mail first, you may end up doing needless work.

Another member suggested an even more efficient approach: senders should retract all messages that are no longer relevant. That would actually reduce the volume of mail and potential confusion.

IT WORKS BOTH WAYS

In an earlier article we mentioned the phenomenon of the memorable experience. Several members wrote to remind us that the effect works both ways. Our article only mentioned that a single bad experience can distort an otherwise good experience. We failed to acknowledge that a single, unexpectedly good experience can be the "story" that is told about us again and again.

A small kindness, a genuine expression of understanding, a sympathetic ear, or helping a lost person find the way can make all the difference.

It's All About The Relationship

"I'm not sure I agree with the Breakfast Club's article about Managing by Walking Around," announced a member as he joined our meeting.

He continued, "I tried it and got strange looks from my team members. I think they were curious, even suspicious, about my presence."

We talked about his experience, and he concluded he may have missed the point. Relationships, not visibility, are the purpose. And relationships are developed by asking open-ended questions about professional goals, personal interests, the work environment, and hobbies. Genuinely listening to answers is a must.

Of course, it isn't done like an inquisition or in one or two sessions. We agreed it's more like getting to know a new neighbor than it is getting to know your daughter's new boyfriend!

⌘

Keep It Down, Please.

We held our last Breakfast Club meeting in a different conference room. About five minutes into the meeting, someone closed the conference room door. No doubt, we were disturbing them.

As a result of that subtle reminder, we developed this quiz:

All other things being equal, the environment determines how far sound travels. Which conversation travels farthest, one

- on a still lake.
- within an office with the door open.
- over a frozen lake.
- on a cell phone.
- in an office hallway.
- on a speakerphone.

Based on several notes we've recently received about distractions in the workplace, many of our members believe office conversations defy the laws of physics and magically increase in volume and distance traveled.

The Breakfast Club team promised one another to be sensitive to just how far belly laughs and conversations travel. We also agreed that an "open door" policy doesn't mean that the office door must always be open.

⌘

Our new Breakfast Club intern sat quietly at last week's team meeting and listened as the others discussed the differences between management and leadership. "What are the definitions of management and leadership?" he asked.

Like any group of teachers, we complimented him on his insightful question. We then, of course, suggested he come to the next meeting with two of the most concise definitions he could find. Here they are:

> Management:
> "Knowing what to do, knowing how to do it, and doing it."
>
> > - Peter Drucker

> Leadership:
> "The art of accomplishing more than the science of management says is possible."
>
> > - Colin Powell

❧

LIKE – NO, CARE – YES

"I'm afraid I don't like the new person who just began reporting to me," announced a member as she joined our meeting.

"So, you expect to like everyone?" was the hypothetical question posed by our team's tough guy. "If you do, get ready for many disappointments," he added.

Our tough guy explained himself, and we found he wasn't as tough as he seemed. He didn't like everyone but he cared for them. He explained that genuinely caring for his team members, sometimes even with tough love, was the most effective thing he could do for the organization, the team members, and himself.

Caring means sometimes:

- encouraging an associate toward personal and professional development
- being a "Dutch Uncle" when missteps or policy violations are made
- celebrating individual or team successes
- being tactfully frank about performance
- being a good listener

- patiently watching a team member struggle with a doable task while resisting the temptation to interfere
- overlooking foibles
- helping a poor performer find a job that better suits his or her talents
- taking joy in seeing others succeed and "leave the nest" for better opportunities

We agreed it is a high wire act to balance the needs of the organization with concern for associates. We concluded it is pointless to fake caring; we will be caught. We also agreed we cannot truly lead without a sense of caring.

"If I had to manage people I neither liked nor cared for, I'd be in the wrong job," our tough guy concluded as he left the meeting.

⌒⌒⌒

Lotta Action – Getting Anything Done?
"Gosh, I was busy around the house on Saturday," announced a member as he joined our meeting.

"Did you actually get anything done?" asked another member.

"Very little," was the sheepish reply.

Our busy person described a Saturday that went like this:

- 9 a.m.: while wife is visiting her parents, I'll surprise her and paint the bedroom
- Go to garage to get paint and other supplies (bought the stuff four months ago)
- Garage looks a little messy, clean it up a bit
- Put the garage door up and notice the mail has arrived
- Hmm, mailbox is very old and weather beaten
- Decide to replace it
- Off to the "Big Box" store for a new mailbox
- Studied the new lawnmowers
- Roamed through the power tools department
- Watched a live demonstration on how to build a deck
- Decided I need an electronic level and bought one
- Went home to determine if all the pictures in the house are level
- Device needs batteries
- Spend fifteen minutes trying to find good batteries
- First picture checked is not level
- Just remembered, forgot to buy mailbox
- Off to a different "Big Box" to see their mailbox selection

- Off to a neighborhood hardware store to see their mailbox selection
- Decide not to buy mailbox—need wife's opinion
- On the way home stopped for a late lunch
- Stopped to get gas and check air pressure in tires
- Tires look worn
- Off to tire store to price new tires
- Off to another tire store for comparison shopping
- Tires a bit pricey—better wait for a sale
- Home again
- Picked up the mail and noticed several bills
- Wrote checks and put envelopes in mailbox for mail carrier to pick up
- Sure do need a new mailbox
- 5:00 p.m. and wife returns home
- I'm exhausted but wife not sympathetic

During bouts of laughter, we agreed that time at the office can easily be spent the same way—much action, little results.

> *Do not tell me how hard you work, tell me how much you get done.*
>
> - James J. Ling

⌘

LUDDITE CLARIFIED

In a previous article we wondered what a Luddite was. We received these good answers:

> *Luddism is the fear of change brought on by advanced technology.*
>
> *The term Luddite has been resurrected from a previous era to describe one who distrusts or fears the inevitable changes brought about by new technology. The original Luddite revolt occurred in 1811, an action against the English Textile factories that displaced craftsmen in favor of machines. Today's Luddites continue to raise moral and ethical arguments against the excesses of modern technology to the extent that our inventions and our technical systems have evolved to control us rather than to serve us and to the extent that such leviathans can threaten our essential humanity.*

> *Someone who is stuck in the past, doesn't like all the "new-fangled technology."*

Editor's Note:

Ned Ludd was an English laborer who was supposed to have destroyed weaving machinery around 1779. Hence the term.

We also received some incorrect, hopefully tongue-in-cheek, answers from members who will remain anonymous:

- What bowling balls are made of.
- The secret ingredient in Sears weather beater paint.
- Crystallized salt formations found in caves caused by seeping ground water.
- What the L. stands for in President James L. Polk's name.
- Game of chance played in Nepal with dice carved from the tusk of a Musk Ox.
- A chemical used to clean fine fabrics.
- The tool a mechanic uses to remove the lud nuts from an automobile wheel.

సింగ్

MONKEY ON MY BACK

"Can everyone see the three monkeys on my back," asked a member as he joined our meeting.

After our quizzical looks subsided, he informed us that one of the *Harvard Business Review's* most popular articles was about "subordinate-imposed time." The authors used an analogy in which a subordinate takes a task (the monkey) off their back and puts it on the boss's back. It's done in a variety of ways. Perhaps the most common is one in which the subordinate opens the conversation with "We've got a problem." What's likely to happen is the monkey is moved from the subordinate to the boss's back.

Managers who can't control the monkey population find themselves running out of time while their subordinates find themselves running out of work.

P.S.: "See Management Time: Who's Got the Monkey?" published in the *Harvard Business Review*, January 1990.

సింగ్

MULTI-TASKING

"I spent Super Bowl weekend zero-tasking," proudly announced a member as he joined our meeting.

After humorous comments like "What's new?" and "Like another day at the office?" subsided, we turned our attention to multitasking.

Although the term had long been used in the technology world, in the late 1990s it began to be applied to human activities. The term implies that, as companies try to "do more with less" and as information grows at a staggering rate, humans need to do several complicated things at once.

Most of us can walk and chew gum at the same time, but researchers believe thoughtful actions such as decision-making must be performed one at a time. They believe that our brain has inherent limitations for processing information during multitasking. David E. Meyer, director of the University of Michigan's Brain, Cognition, and Action Laboratory states, "If you're trying to listen to someone speak while you're writing an e-mail, you might only get the gist, but not the details, of what's being said."

The team then entertained one another with examples of multi-tasking in the workplace: checking e-mail while in a meeting; stepping out of a meeting to take a phone call—or worse, taking the phone call in the meeting; typing e-mail while on the speaker phone; and talking on the phone while driving a car.

> *The greatest gift you can give another is the purity of your attention.*
>
> - Richard Moss

~~~

MUTUAL RESPECT

"My daughter-in-law, the pilot, was in town this weekend, and I had the chance to talk to her about that industry's incredible safety record," announced a member as she joined us.

She went on to say the aviation culture is collegial and every team member shares responsibility for solving problems and preventing errors.

We agreed that errors are reduced when all team members work collegially toward common goals. The leader expects team participation and listens before making decisions. And team members are assertive but with respect.

> *Listen to your experts - the people on the front line.*
> - Karl E. Weick, Organizational Psychologist

Oops – I Did It Again!

"Yikes," announced a manager as he joined our meeting. "I made what I thought was a straightforward decision, and I've spent the last three days dealing with the confusion I've created."

"You know," said the member who is reading *Classic Drucker*, "Peter Drucker said a decision has not been made until people know four things."

The showoff then rattled off the four things:

- the name of the person accountable for carrying it out
- the deadline
- the names of the people who will be affected by the decision and therefore have to know about, understand, and approve it—or at least not be strongly opposed to it
- the names of the people who have to be informed of the decision, even if they are not directly affected by it.

We agreed a good communication plan must be part of every decision.

∽⌒∼

Problem Solved

We received a number of creative solutions to a previous article's brain-teaser. The generally agreed upon answer: Turn the car over to the friend who once saved your life so he can drive the sick woman to the hospital. You take the bus with the partner of your dreams.

Speaking of creativity, a few articles ago we spoke of inertia. A member sent us this "motivator": Always remember if you have to swallow a frog, the longer you stare at it, the harder it will be. He went on to say, "This isn't original but it's always worked for me."

∽⌒∼

Problem Solving

In one of our meetings, we asked ourselves "What is the first step to solving a problem?" We generated these ideas:

- Make sure there is a problem
- Hope it goes away
- Collect data

- Tell your boss
- Determine the root cause
- Don't tell your boss
- Clearly define the problem
- Identify the problem owner
- Form a committee
- Find someone to blame

The first step towards the solution to any problem is optimism.
- John Baines

∽∾∾

PUT MULTI-TASKING ON HOLD

We received several thoughtful comments about our article on multi-tasking. A consistent theme was that fast-paced lives make it tempting, almost necessary, to multi-task, but we must do it judiciously. For instance, we may be able to make tea and fry eggs at the same time. But it's not a good idea to assume one can multi-task while involved in critical thinking, such as developing a patient's treatment plan. In fact, it's a good idea to hang a "do not disturb" sign when trying to perform important critical thinking.

It's also time to hit the multi-task "hold button" when a loved one or colleague needs to "talk." As Richard Moss said: "The greatest gift you can give another is the purity of your attention."

∽∾∾

QUIET TIME

We received comments about our article on "quiet time." One member had used the technique but fell out of the habit. She plans to start again. Some members think it is a worthwhile, but impractical idea. One argued that it is next to impossible for "front line" managers to schedule it. Although we understand and sympathize, we wonder if "quiet time" would eventually help decrease the number of day-to-day crises. Just as lumberjacks make time to sharpen their saws, perhaps we must take time to sharpen our management skills and tactics.

One member used the word "self-discipline." At first we thought she was suggesting that we should discipline ourselves to work harder or longer. On the contrary, she recommends we use self-discipline to force ourselves to make time for thinking, planning, and mindfully working on important, not urgent, things.

It reminds us of advice financial planners give. "Pay yourself first," they say, "by using payroll deduction to automatically save ten percent of your earnings."

⌒⌒⌒

SLOW DOWN, YOU MOVE TOO FAST!

"Seems like my summer weekends are so busy that I look forward to Monday," announced a member as she joined our meeting. "But," she continued, "weekdays seem just as hectic."

Commiseration filled the room and eventually the book *The Hurried Woman Syndrome* by Brent W. Bost, M.D., came up. Everyone in the room agreed that stress and hurrying in everything we do is the norm.

We didn't have any quick answers, but someone did share these words by Jean-Louis Seven-Schreiber: "What I fear most about stress is not that it kills, but that it prevents one from savoring life."

Being in a constant hurry isn't new. Over fifty years ago this was a line in a popular movie: "What happened to all the time we saved by taking the helicopter?" Know which movie? No fair using Google!

P.S.: Lest our younger readers feel left out, there was a remake in 1995.

⌒⌒⌒

SPEAK UP – IT'S IMPORTANT

"I think a bad decision was made in the meeting I just left," announced a member as she joined us.

"Did you speak up?" asked another member.

"I'm embarrassed to say that I didn't," was the sheepish answer.

That reminded us of the Challenger explosion. You may recall that an engineer urged NASA officials to call off the launch.

According to *The Erickson Tribune*, McDonald states:

> *There were a dozen other engineers who supported my argument that night, but not one of them spoke up. In my discussions with many of them, I found that when management hears one or two people alone, they discount their opinion. Had the whole group said they didn't support the decision to launch, I think that would have dramatically changed minds.*

He also states "Everybody's going to be wrong sometimes, but it's your professional responsibility to voice your opinion, right or wrong."

ᑫᔑᕐᓭᓪ

STRESS-FREE WORKPLACE

In a previous article we discussed fun at work. We received this response from a member:

> *Our associate surveys reveal that stress or the perception of a stressful work environment is a concern to many of us. Having "fun at work" and feeling valued for the work performed may be an effective strategy to reduce stress and improve morale. We spend a good portion of our life at work—if work is not enjoyable it will not only affect our morale but our health as well.*

And these thoughts from another member:

> *People work best when they feel they are of value to a job. If the environment is positive and people are free to express themselves they feel their input is appreciated and valued.*

A few other words of wisdom:

> *Business should be fun. Without fun, people are left wearing emotional raincoats most of their working lives. Building fun into business is vital; it brings life into our daily being. Fun is a powerful motive for most of our activities and should be a direct part of our livelihood. We should not relegate it to something we buy after work with money we earn.*
>
> - Michael Phillips

> *What I fear most about stress is not that it kills, but that it pre-vents one from savoring life.*
>
> - Jean-Louis Seven-Schreiber

> *Work is much more fun than fun.*
>
> - Noel Coward

ᑫᔑᕐᓭᓪ

TELL ME WHAT'S HAPPENING

"I learned something from road construction workers," announced a member as she joined our meeting.

"You mean the people who have traffic backed up on half the streets in the area?" cracked another commuter.

"They're putting new pipes under the street not far from my home, and last night I noticed a new sign. It said something like 'Road Construction. Long Delays Possible.'

"Somehow that warning made the waits more tolerable. I appreciated the warning if the wait was long, and felt lucky if the wait was short."

We agreed that patients also appreciate information that helps with their expectations. If a procedure must be delayed, it helps to not only inform the patient but to give a reason. Something like "An emergency case just arrived. We know waiting is difficult and we're sorry, but it looks like you may have a twenty-minute wait" is better than saying nothing and allowing the patient to wonder if they've been forgotten.

⚯

THE 80/20 RULE?

"I just returned from a heart-to-heart conversation with an associate who reminded me, once again, that she is irritated by those who do not share her intense work ethic," said a member as she joined our meeting.

"I said the team was lucky to have an overachiever like her. She said she was not an overachiever, it's just that the others were underachievers."

"That's a common perception of those who are highly productive. I suspect your employee expects everyone to be just like her."

Another member added, "It sounds like she takes it personally that she must work with what she sees as slackers."

We agreed that it is easy for overachievers to see themselves as just regular workers. We also agreed that it helps to remind exceptional workers that they are, indeed, exceptional. We must also remind them that variation exists in all facets of life. Some people are taller than others. Some are morning people. Some are shy. And some people simply work harder than others. It is the nature of things and, difficult as it is, we must accept it without rancor.

I only know one truth: work alone makes you happy. And this sole truth of which I am certain, I am always forgetting.
- Jules Renard

⚯

THINK FIRST – ACT SECOND

"My father graciously spent the weekend helping me finish my basement," announced a member as she joined our meeting. "He's a carpenter, and I enjoyed watching him effortlessly use all the tools he brought with him."

"So, what did you learn?" asked the woodworker in the group.

"Measure twice, cut once!" was the quick reply.

Those who were not familiar with the advice marveled at its wisdom. We wondered how it could be applied to an office environment. We entertained one another with horror stories about quickly composing an e-mail message and then retracting it or sending a second one to explain the first one.

We agreed on this advice to e-mail users: "Read twice, send once."

~~~

TIME FOR A NEW MOVIE

As she joined our last meeting, a member announced, "My husband got a new boss about three months ago, and it seems he complains about him every night at dinner. When I asked him if the new boss had any redeeming values, he quickly came up with quite a few. I summoned the nerve to suggest he ponder those now and then."

The team then discussed our propensity to play over and over again mental "stories" or "movies." For instance, we form a snap opinion about our new boss, and it's probably based on emotions rather than facts. We never really challenge the initial perception. Instead, we habitually play the "bad boss movie."

We agreed it helps to be aware of our mental movies and to change reels regularly.

~~~

TIME WITH OTHERS

In his book *Happiness, Lessons from a New Science*, economist Richard Layard included a table (imagine that) presenting the level of happiness we experience while interacting with different people. Here it is:

Interacting With	Average Happiness
Friends	3.7
Relatives	3.4
Spouse/partner	3.3

My children	3.3
Clients/customers	2.8
Co-workers	2.8
Alone	2.7
???????????????	2.4

Whose company do we typically consider worse than being alone? Hint: It begins with the letter B.

～⌒～

WALKING AND THINKING AND WALKING

"My wife was almost run over while on her business trip to England," mentioned a member as he joined our meeting.

"Crazy English drivers?" asked another member.

"No, she looked to her left for oncoming traffic but was almost hit by a car coming from the right. She forgot they drive on the left in England."

That prompted a conversation about hall and elevator etiquette. We agreed many of us are absent-minded or in such a hurry that we walk on the left and even try to get on an elevator before others have had a chance to get off.

We agreed it is especially important to be careful when walking in hospital corridors. We also agreed "traveling" is a great time to simply clear our mind and concentrate on the walk itself.

～⌒～

WELCOME YOUR NEW RECRUIT

"Disappointment on the home front," announced a member as she joined our meeting. She continued, "After one day at a new job, my college-educated twenty-two-year-old daughter announced she is starting a new job search."

"Not uncommon," contributed another member. "About twenty percent of new hires consider doing the same thing after just one day on the job. Research indicates new hires often just don't feel welcomed."

Many in the meeting could relate and shared horror stories like being told, "Oh, I thought you were starting next week—we're not ready for you." Or not having a single co-worker stop by and "show her the ropes." Or eating alone for the first two weeks. Or not having office supplies. Or not even being told where the rest room was.

We agreed it's a good idea to treat a new worker as a guest for the first week or so. Perhaps then they won't say, "It's a great place to work, except for the people!"

WELL – EXCUSE ME!

"All I did was ask a simple question and the person seemed to take offense," remarked a team member as he joined our meeting.

"How did you ask the question?" queried another member.

All I said was, "Why do you do it that way?"

After the groans subsided, we discussed the impact questions can have. We agreed they can quite often be intimidating, even irritating. An example we all can relate to is the parent who challenges the teenager who arrives home an hour late. "I worry about you when you're late!" often works better than "Where were you!"

❦

WHAT – ME, WORRY?

"I think I'm raising a worry wart," announced a member as she joined our meeting. "My twelve-year-old daughter is obsessed with global warming. She's convinced next summer's average temperature will be one-hundred fifty degrees."

That got us to talking about worry. We agreed it's common to worry now and then. From time to time we all worry about family, health, job, and other personal issues. And some of us, like the young lady mentioned above, worry about issues facing the entire world.

Sometimes, though, worry becomes a problem. It can disrupt our daily routine, hamper our ability to focus at work, or keep us from getting enough sleep. These can fatigue us to the point where we have no energy to live in the present moment.

If worry begins to control your life, seek help.

> *I am an old man and have known a great many troubles, but most of them never happened.*
> - Mark Twain

❦

WHAT ARE YOU TAKING FOR GRANTED?

"Story time," announced a member as she joined our meeting. She continued, "I attended a sixtieth wedding anniversary celebration, and of course, someone asked the wife for the secret to such a long and happy marriage."

She told the gathering that "in her day" Monday was laundry day. She used a wringer washer and had no dryer. As she hung clothes on the line in the backyard, she developed the habit of asking herself, "What am I taking for granted?"

Needless to say, such a question gave her a valuable perspective on many aspects of life.

We agreed that asking ourselves that question specifically about our world of work is a wise idea.

⌀⌀

WHERE DID THE TIME GO?

"Sabrina" was the movie we alluded to in a previous article. The setting: a busy, wealthy, type A, male executive suggests to his female guest that they take a helicopter to the airport to save time. As they fly in a private jet, they hold this conversation:

> Sabrina: Don't you ever look out the window?
> Linus Larrabee: When do I have time?
> Sabrina: What happened to all that time we saved taking the helicopter?
> Linus Larrabee: I'm storing it up.
> Sabrina: No, you're not.

The Breakfast Club team agreed that hurrying from one activity to another or constantly thinking about what we are going to do next deprives us of the present moment. Which, of course, is the only moment we ever really have.

Perhaps Alain said it best: "There ought to be signs put up all around, and in all languages, saying open your eyes, and enjoy."

⌀⌀

WHO DOES THAT?

In one of our articles we talked about the importance of recognizing associates for work that too often and too easily goes unnoticed.

A member sent us the following "Dilbert-like" motto:

Nobody notices what I do 'til I don't do it!

⌀⌀

WHO PACKED YOUR CHUTE?

Breakfast Club obtained permission from Charlie Plumb (www.charlieplumb. com) to share the following story. We think it is especially appropriate for those of us in health care.

Recently, I was sitting in a restaurant in Kansas City. A man about two tables away kept looking at me. I didn't recognize him. A few minutes into our meal he stood up and walked over to my table, looked down at me, pointed his finger in my face and said, "You're Captain Plumb."

I looked up and I said, "Yes sir, I'm Captain Plumb."

He said, "You flew jet fighters in Vietnam. You were on the aircraft carrier Kitty Hawk. You were shot down. You parachuted into enemy hands and spent six years as a prisoner of war."

I said, "How in the world did you know all that?"

He replied, "Because, I packed your parachute."

I was speechless. I staggered to my feet and held out a very grateful hand of thanks. This guy came up with just the proper words. He grabbed my hand, he pumped my arm and said, "I guess it worked."

"Yes sir, indeed it did," I said, "and I must tell you I've said a lot of prayers of thanks for your nimble fingers, but I never thought I'd have the opportunity to express my gratitude in person."

He said, "Were all the panels there?"

"Well sir, I must shoot straight with you," I said, "of the eighteen panels that were supposed to be in that parachute, I had fifteen good ones. Three were torn, but it wasn't your fault, it was mine. I jumped out of that jet fighter at a high rate of speed, close to the ground. That's what tore the panels in the chute. It wasn't the way you packed it.

"Let me ask you a question," I said, "do you keep track of all the parachutes you pack?"

"No," he responded, "it's enough gratification for me just to know that I've served."

I didn't get much sleep that night. I kept thinking about that man. I kept wondering what he might have looked like in a Navy uniform—a Dixie cup hat, a bib in the back and bell bottom trousers. I wondered how many times I might have passed him on board the Kitty Hawk. I wondered how many times I might have seen him and not even said "good morning," "how are you," or anything because, you see, I was a fighter pilot and he was just a sailor. How many hours did he spend on that long wooden table in the bowels of that ship weaving the shrouds and folding the silks of those chutes? I could have cared less...until one day my parachute came along and he packed it for me.

So the philosophical question here is this: How's your parachute packing coming along? Who looks to you for strength in times of need? And perhaps, more importantly, who are the special people in your life who provide you the encouragement you need when the chips are down? Perhaps it's time right now to give those people a call and thank them for packing your chute.

~∽∾~

WHO SCORED THAT GOAL?

A story about a Little League soccer coach:

After the games I would ask a question like, "Who scored that first goal?" Initially one boy would raise his hand and I would respond, "No! We all scored that goal. Every person on a team is responsible for scoring a goal. The individual who touches it last is the one who may get the statistic, but scoring a goal starts with the goalie passing to a defender, who passes to a midfielder, who passes to a forward. If the forward scores, it is because of everyone else on the team, not just him.

"Now, who scored that goal?" All the athletes would raise their hands. All of them received credit for each goal scored.

P.S.: This story can be found in the book *Dr. Deming The American Who Taught the Japanese About Quality* by Rafael Aguayo.

~∽∾~

WOULDN'T YOU LIKE TO KNOW?

During one of our meetings, a member told this true story:

The primary duty of a purchasing clerk was to order parts that were used to make large, expensive machines. He purchased parts based on how many machines were sold in the previous two months.

His employer informed its customers that it was going to discontinue selling one of its machines and deplete its inventory of them.

Customers who liked that model suddenly placed many orders for it. The purchasing clerk was alarmed by the sudden increase in sales. He immediately went on a buying spree and "stocked up" on all kinds of costly parts for future production.

After the company discontinued the model, they discovered they had about a ten-year supply of worthless parts tucked away in a warehouse.

You can guess who wasn't told about the plans to discontinue the model!

We agreed every project should have a "Who Else Needs to Know" list.

www.ingramcontent.com/pod-product-compliance
Lightning Source LLC
Chambersburg PA
CBHW060608200326
41521CB00007B/704